77 Genetic
Eng. Quote

SPORT + Responsibility

LIFE IS A MIRACLE

LIFE IS A MIRACLE

AN ESSAY AGAINST MODERN SUPERSTITION

WENDELL BERRY

COUNTERPOINT

WASHINGTON, D.C.

Library of Congress Catalog Card Number: 00-028249
ISBN: 1-58243-058-6

FIRST PRINTING

Jacket and text design by David Bullen

Printed in the United States of America on acid-free paper
that meets the American National Standards
Institute z39-48 Standard.

COUNTERPOINT
P.O. Box 65793
Washington, D.C. 20035-5793

Counterpoint is a member of the Perseus Books Group

10 9 8 7 6 5 4 3 2 1

In memory:
Lionel Basney (1946–1999)

"We are not getting something for nothing.
We are getting nothing for everything."

Contents

Thy life's a miracle. Speak yet again.

King Lear, IV, vi, 55

LIFE IS A MIRACLE

1. Ignorance

THE EXPRESSED dissatisfaction of some scientists with the dangerous oversimplifications of commercialized science has encouraged me to hope that this dissatisfaction will run its full course. These scientists, I hope, will not stop with some attempt at a merely theoretical or technical "correction," but will press on toward a new, or a renewed, propriety in the study and the use of the living world.

No such change is foreseeable in the terms of the presently dominant mechanical explanations of things. Such a change is imaginable only if we are willing to risk an unfashionable recourse to our cultural tradition. Human hope may always have resided in our ability, in time of need, to return to our cultural landmarks and reorient ourselves.

One of the principle landmarks of the course of my own life is

Shakespeare's tragedy of *King Lear*. Over the last forty-five years I have returned to *King Lear* many times. Among the effects of that play—on me, and I think on anybody who reads it closely—is the recognition that in all our attempts to renew or correct ourselves, to shake off despair and have hope, our starting place is always and only our experience. We can begin (and we must always be beginning) only where our history has so far brought us, with what we have done.

Lately my thoughts about the inevitably commercial genetic manipulations already in effect or contemplated have sent me back to *King Lear* again. The whole play is about kindness, both in the usual sense, and in the sense of truth-to-kind, naturalness, or knowing the limits of our specifically *human* nature. But this issue is dealt with most explicitly in an episode of the subplot, in which the Earl of Gloucester is recalled from despair so that he may die in his full humanity.

The old earl has been blinded in retribution for his loyalty to the king, and in this fate he sees a kind of justice for, as he says, "I stumbled when I saw" (*King Lear*, The Pelican Shakespeare, IV, i, 19). He, like Lear, is guilty of hubris or presumption, of treating life as knowable, predictable, and within his control. He has falsely accused and driven away his loyal son, Edgar. Exiled and under sentence of death, Edgar has disguised himself as a madman and beggar. He becomes, in that role, the guide of his blinded father, who asks to be led to Dover where he intends to kill himself by leaping off a cliff. Edgar's task is to save his father from despair, and he succeeds, for Gloucester dies at last "'Twixt two extremes of passion, joy and grief . . ." (V, iii, 199). He dies, that is, within the proper bounds of the human estate. Edgar does not want his father to give up on life. To give up on life is to pass beyond the possibility of change or redemption. And so he does not lead his father to the cliff's verge, but only *tells* him he has done so. Gloucester renounces the world, blesses Edgar, his supposedly absent son, and, according to the stage direction, "Falls forward and swoons" (IV, vi, 41).

When he returns to consciousness, Edgar now speaks to him in the guise of a passer-by at the bottom of the cliff, from which he pretends to have seen Gloucester fall. Here he assumes explicitly the role of spiritual guide to his father.

Gloucester, dismayed to find himself still alive, attempts to refuse help: "Away, and let me die" (IV, vi, 48).

And then Edgar, after an interval of several lines in which he represents himself as a stranger, speaks the filial (and fatherly) line about which my thoughts have gathered:

> Thy life's a miracle. Speak yet again.
>
> (IV, vi, 55)

This is the line that calls Gloucester back—out of hubris, and the damage and despair that invariably follow—into the properly subordinated human life of grief and joy, where change and redemption are possible.

The power of that line read in the welter of innovation and speculation of the bioengineers will no doubt be obvious. One immediately recognizes that suicide is not the only way to give up on life. We know that creatures and kinds of creatures can be killed, deliberately or inadvertently. And most farmers know that any creature that is sold has in a sense been given up on; there is a big difference between selling this year's lamb crop, which is, as such, all that it can be, and selling the breeding flock or the farm, which hold the immanence of a limitless promise.

*

A little harder to compass is the danger that we can give up on life also by presuming to "understand" it—that is by reducing it to the *terms* of our understanding and by treating it as predictable or mechanical. The most radical influence of reductive science has been the virtually universal adoption of the idea that the world, its creatures, and all the parts of its creatures are machines—that is, that there is no difference between creature and artifice, birth and manufacture, thought and computation. Our language, wherever it is used, is now almost invariably conditioned by the assumption that fleshly bodies are machines full of mechanisms, fully compatible with the mechanisms of medicine, industry, and commerce; and that minds are computers fully compatible with electronic technology.

This may have begun as a metaphor, but in the language as it is used (and as it affects industrial practice) it has evolved from metaphor through equation to identification. And this usage institutionalizes the human wish, or the sin of wishing, that life might be, or might be made to be, predictable.

I have read of Werner Heisenberg's principle that "Whenever one treats living organisms as physiochemical systems they must necessarily behave as such." I am not competent to have an opinion about the truth of that. I do feel able to say that whenever one treats living organisms as machines they must necessarily be *perceived* to behave as such. And I can see that the proposition is reversible: Whenever one perceives living organisms as machines they must necessarily be treated as such. William Blake made the same point earlier in this age of reduction and affliction:

> What seems to Be, Is, To those to whom
> It seems to Be, & is productive of the most dreadful
> Consequences to those to whom it seems to Be ...
> (Blake, *Complete Writings,* Oxford, 1966, p. 663)

For quite a while it has been possible for a free and thoughtful person to see that to treat life as mechanical or predictable or understandable is to reduce it. Now, almost suddenly, it is becoming clear that to reduce life to the scope of our understanding (whatever "model" we use) is inevitably to enslave it, make property of it, and put it up for sale.

This is to give up on life, to carry it beyond change and redemption, and to increase the proximity of despair.

Cloning—to use the most obvious example—is not a way to improve sheep. On the contrary, it is a way to stall the sheep's lineage and make it unimprovable. No true breeder could consent to it, for true breeders have their farm and their market in mind, and always are trying to breed a better sheep. Cloning, besides being a new method of sheep-stealing, is only a pathetic attempt to make sheep predictable. But this is an affront to reality. As any shepherd would know, the scientist who thinks he has made sheep predictable has only made himself eligible to be outsmarted.

The same sort of limitation and depreciation is involved in the proposed cloning of fetuses for body parts, and in other extreme measures for prolonging individual lives. No individual life is an end in itself. One can live fully only by participating fully in the succession of the generations, in death as well as in life. Some would say (and I am one of them) that we can live fully only by making ourselves as answerable to the claims of eternity as to those of time.

The problem, as it appears to me, is that we are using the wrong language. The language we use to speak of the world and its creatures, including ourselves, has gained a certain analytical power (along with a lot of expertish pomp) but has lost much of its power to designate *what* is being analyzed or to convey any respect or care or affection or devotion toward it. As a result we have a lot of genuinely concerned people calling upon us to "save" a world which their language simultaneously reduces to an assemblage of perfectly featureless and dispirited "ecosystems," "organisms," "environments," "mechanisms," and the like. It is impossible to prefigure the salvation of the world in the same language by which the world has been dismembered and defaced.

By almost any standard, it seems to me, the reclassification of the world from creature to machine must involve at least a perilous reduction of moral complexity. So must the shift in our attitude toward the creation from reverence to understanding. So must the shift in our perceived relationship to nature from that of steward to that of absolute owner, manager, and engineer. So even must our permutation of "holy" to "holistic."

At this point I can only declare myself. I think that the poet and scholar Kathleen Raine was correct in reminding us that life, like holiness, can be known only by being experienced (*The Inner*

Journey of the Poet, Braziller, 1982, pp. 180–181). To experience it is not to "figure it out" or even to understand it, but to suffer it and rejoice in it as it is. In suffering it and rejoicing in it as it is, we know that we do not and cannot understand it completely. We know, moreover, that we do not wish to have it appropriated by somebody's claim to have understood it. Though we have life, it is beyond us. We do not know how we have it, or why. We do not know what is going to happen to it, or to us. It is not predictable; though we can destroy it, we cannot make it. It cannot, except by reduction and the grave risk of damage, be controlled. It is, as Blake said, holy. To think otherwise is to enslave life, and to make, not humanity, but a few humans its predictably inept masters.

We need a new Emancipation Proclamation, not for a specific race or species, but for life itself—and that, I believe, is precisely what Edgar urges upon his once presumptuous and now desperate father:

> Thy life's a miracle. Speak yet again.

Gloucester's attempted suicide is really an attempt to recover control over his life—a control he believes (mistakenly) that he once had and has lost:

> O you mighty gods!
> This world I do renounce, and in your sights
> Shake patiently my great affliction off.
>
> (IV, vi, 34–36)

The nature of his despair is delineated in his belief that he can control his life by killing himself, which is a paradox we will meet again three and a half centuries later at the extremity of industrial warfare when we believed that we could "save" by means of destruction.

Later, under the guidance of his son, Gloucester prays a prayer that is exactly opposite to his previous one—

> You ever-gentle gods, take my breath from me;
> Let not my worser spirit tempt me again
> To die before you please
>
> (IV, vi, 213-215)

—in which he renounces control over his life. He has given up his life as an understood possession, and has taken it back as miracle and mystery. And his reclamation as a human being is acknowledged in Edgar's response: "Well pray you, father" (IV, vi, 215).

It seems clear that humans cannot significantly reduce or mitigate the dangers inherent in their use of life by accumulating more information or better theories or by achieving greater predictability or more caution in their scientific and industrial work. To treat life as less than a miracle is to give up on it.

*

I am aware how brash this commentary will seem, coming from me, who have no competence or learning in science. The issue I am attempting to deal with, however, is not knowledge but ignorance. In ignorance I believe I may pronounce myself a fair expert.

One of our problems is that we humans cannot live without acting; we *have* to act. Moreover, we *have* to act on the basis of what we know, and what we know is incomplete. What we have come to know so far is demonstrably incomplete, since we keep on learning more, and there seems little reason to think that our knowledge will become significantly more complete. The mystery surrounding our life probably is not significantly reducible. And so the question of how to act in ignorance is paramount.

Our history enables us to suppose that it may be all right to act on the basis of incomplete knowledge *if* our culture has an effective way of telling us that our knowledge is incomplete, and also of telling us how to act in our state of ignorance. We may go so far as to say that it is all right to act on the basis of sure knowledge, since our studies and our experience have given us knowledge that seems to be pretty sure. But apparently it is dangerous to act on the assumption that sure knowledge is complete knowledge—or on the assumption that our knowledge will increase fast enough to outrace the bad consequences of the arrogant use of incomplete knowledge. To trust "progress" or our putative "genius" to solve all the problems that we cause is worse than bad science; it is bad religion.

A second human problem is that evil exists and is an ever-present and lively possibility. We know that malevolence is always ready to appropriate the means that we have intended for good. For example, the technical means that have industrialized agriculture, making it (by very limited standards) more efficient and productive and easy, have also made it more toxic, more violent, and more vulnerable—have made it, in fact, far less dependable if not less predictable than it used to be.

One kind of evil certainly is the willingness to destroy what we cannot make—life, for instance—and we have greatly enlarged our means of doing that. And what are we to do? Must we let evil and our implication in it drive us to despair?

The present course of reductive science—as when we allow agriculture to be invaded by the technology of war and the economics of industrialism—*is* driving us to despair, as witness the incidence of suicide among farmers.

If we lack the cultural means to keep incomplete knowledge from becoming the basis of arrogant and dangerous behavior, then the intellectual disciplines themselves become dangerous. What is the point of the further study of nature if that leads to the further destruction of nature? To study the "purpose" of the organ within the organism or of the organism within the ecosystem is *still* reductive if we do so with the assumption that we will or can finally figure it out. This simply captures the world as the subject of present or future "understanding," which will become the basis of further industrial and commercial optimism, which will become the basis of further exploitation and destruction of communities, ecosystems, and local cultures.

I am not of course proposing an end to science and other intellectual disciplines, but rather a change of standards and goals. The standards of our behavior must be derived, not from the capability of technology, but from the nature of places and communities. We must shift the priority from production to local adaptation, from innovation to familiarity, from power to elegance, from costliness to thrift. We must learn to think about propriety in scale and design, as determined by human and ecological health. By such changes we might again make our work an answer to despair.

II. Propriety

MY GENERAL concern is with what I take to be the increasing inability of the scientific, artistic, and religious disciplines to help us address the issue of propriety in our thoughts and acts. "Propriety" is an old term, even an old-fashioned one, and is not much in favor. Its value is in its reference to the fact that we are not alone. The idea of propriety makes an issue of the fittingness of our conduct to our place or circumstances, even to our hopes. It acknowledges the always-pressing realities of context and of influence; we cannot speak or act or live out of context. Our life inescapably affects other lives, which inescapably affect our life. We are being measured, in other words, by a standard that we did not make and cannot destroy. It is by that standard, and only by that standard, that we know we are in a crisis in our relationship to nature. The term "environmental crisis," crude and inexact as it is, acknowledges that we have invoked this standard and have measured ourselves by it. A civilization that is destroying all of its sources in nature has raised starkly the issue of propriety, whether or not it wishes to have done so.

Propriety is the antithesis of individualism. To raise the issue of propriety is to deny that any individual's wish is the ultimate measure of the world. The issue presents itself as a set of questions: Where are we? (This question applies, with as much particularity as human competence will allow, to all of the world's millions of small localities.) Who are we? (The proper answer to this question depends on where we are and where we have been, and it includes history.) What is our condition? (This is a *practical* question.) What are our abilities? (This also is a practical question. It refers to abilities that are *proven,* not to abilities that are theoretical or potential, such as "aptitude" or I.Q.) What appropriately may we do in our own interest *here?* (And this question submits to the standard of the health of the place.) These questions address themselves to all the disciplines, but they do not call for specialized answers. They cannot, I think, be answered by specialists—or not, at least, by specialists in isolation from one another.

To ask such questions seriously now is not quite absurd, for the questions are valid and urgent, but it is nonetheless to risk a sort of comedy, for the questions are as foreign to our sciences and arts as presently practiced, and to our institutions of government, learning, and religion, as they are to the global corporations whose existence depends upon their (and our) willingness to ignore any such questions.

All of the disciplines are increasingly identifiable as professionalisms, which are increasingly conformable to the aims and standards of industrialism. All of the disciplines are failing the test of propriety because they are failing the test of locality. The professionals of the disciplines don't *care* where they are. Though they are inescapably in context, they assume or pretend that they think and work without context. They subscribe to the preeminence of the mind and (logically from that) of the career. The questions of propriety, calling as they must for local answers, call necessarily for *small* answers. But small local answers are now as far beneath the notice of professionalism as of commercialism. Professionalism aspires to *big* answers that will make headlines, money, and promotions. It longs, moreover, for answers that are uniform and universal—the same styles, explanations, routines, tools, methods, models, beliefs, amusements, etc., for everybody everywhere. And like the corporations, whose appetite for "growth" seems now ungovernable, the institutions of government, education, and religion are now all too likely to measure their success in terms of size and number. All the institutions seem to have learned to imitate the organizational structures and to adopt the values and aims of industrial corporations. It is astonishing to realize how quickly and shamelessly doctors and lawyers and even college professors have taken to drumming up trade, and how readily hospitals, once run according to the laws of healing, mercy, and charity, have submitted to the laws of professionalism, industrial methodology, careerism, and profit.

This is happening to all the disciplines, but because science is the most influential category of the disciplines, and increasingly has set the pattern for the rest, we must be concerned first of all with science. Stephen Edelglass, Georg Maier, Hans Gebert, and John Davy in their book, *The Marriage of Sense and Thought*, wrote that "Science now functions in society rather as the Church did in the Middle Ages" (p. 16). What kind of religion science is, and how it works as such, are questions we will have to deal with.

*

One used to hear a great deal about "pure science." The universities, one was given to understand, were full of scientists who were disinterestedly pursuing truth. "Pure science" did not permit the scientist to ask so crude and pragmatic a question as *why* this or that truth was being pursued; it was just assumed, not only that to know the truth was good, but that, once the truth was discovered, it would somehow be *used* for good. This is a singularly naive view of science (as it would be of any human enterprise), but it survived at least into the early days of space exploration, when a lot of aficionados of so-called high technology assumed that NASA existed to sponsor voyages of pure discovery: to learn whatever might be learned, to take pictures of the earth and other planets, and to provide extremely expensive mystical experiences to astronauts. Some people believed that this enterprise was really a sort of spiritual quest, and would always remain above the gross concerns of, for example, the military-industrial complex. It would promote instead a renewed tenderness toward our "planet" by such devices as pictures of half of said planet, taken at a distance that reduced it to a blue bauble something like a Christmas tree ornament. In our foolish insistence on substituting technology for vision, we forget that we are not the first to have seen "the whole earth" from such a distance. Dante saw it (*Paradiso XXII*, 133–154) from a higher level of human accomplishment, and at far less economic and ecological cost, several hundred years before NASA.

The possibility of pure science was significantly diminished, surely, by the time early scientists had invented metallurgy and then gunpowder, and it diminished steadily from then on. By now, when the possibilities of application have so enormously multiplied and the greed of corporations has grown so elaborate that they wish to patent discoveries before they have been discovered, it appears safest to assume that all sciences are "applied." Science may at times have been altruistically applied. But even such nominally altruistic sciences as medicine and plant-breeding have now become so deeply interpenetrated with economics and politics that their motives are at best mixed with, and at worst replaced by, the motives of corporations and governments. If nothing else, the increasing costliness of the practice of conventional science, and its consequent dependence on large grants or investments, would mitigate against its purity. One can only assume that pure science now needs to move fast (and beg hard) to keep its skirts from being lifted by the ever randy and handy corporate giants.

*

As I have already confessed, I am not at all a scientist. And yet, like every human inhabitant of the modern world, I have experienced many of the effects (costs and benefits) of science; I have received a great deal of hearsay of it; and I know that I am always under its influence and at its mercy. Though I am unable to comment on its methods or the truth of its discoveries, I am nonetheless appropriately interested in its motives—in what it thinks it is doing and in how it justifies itself. I agree with the proposition that science (or "science-and-technology") has now become a sort of religion; I am aware also that in many ways it rules over us. I want to know by what power it has crowned and mitered itself.

I believe it is generally agreed that "science" means knowledge of a special kind: factual knowledge that can be proven by measure, that can stand up to empirical testing. Scientific knowledge is the hard cash of the modern economy of thought; its worth is constant, no matter who has it; its value is not derived from belief or opinion or speculation or desire. Once established, it cannot be argued about.

Science has to do, famously, with theory. "Theory," at root, is related to the word "theater"; it has to do with watching, with observation. A scientific theory is an aid to observation. It involves assumptions that appear to be consistent with known facts. It is not proven; it is useful because it may lead to evidence or to proofs.

Science also involves prediction. Prediction is a highly disciplined concept when it is used in relation to the methodology of proof: A thing is true only if it is *predictably* true; a thing is true, not because it is true now, but because it is true always. But in the hands of such "scientists" as meteorologists and economists, whose putative usefulness depends directly upon their ability to predict and whose predictions are frequently wrong, the meaning of prediction begins to slide from science toward journalism. The same slide occurs when scientists, on the basis of early results, predict the success of a course of experimentation. Alert readers of newspapers will certainly have noticed the frequency of reports that scientists "may have" discovered something or other, or that new data "may prove" something or other. Journalists, and apparently some scientists also, are partial to news stories beginning "Scientists foresee" or "Scientists predict."

This seems to come from abuse of faith, which is another essential attribute of science. There is a sort of scientific faith that is legitimate. It is hard to see how the work of science could be done if scientists did not have faith in the workability and soundness of their methods. This is not faith of the highest sort, obviously, but is akin to the unproven confidence with which we non-scientists face the unknowns of our own workdays. But under various suasions of profession and personality, this legitimate faith in scientific methodology seems to veer off into a kind of religious faith in the power of science to know all things and solve all problems, whereupon the scientist may become an evangelist and go forth to save the world.

This religification and evangelizing of science, in defiance of scientific principles, is now commonplace and is widely accepted or tolerated by people who are not scientists. We really seem to have conceded to scientists, to the extent of their own regrettable willingness to occupy it, the place once occupied by the prophets and priests of religion. This can have happened only because of a general abdication of our responsibility to be critical and, above all, self-critical.

Why is there not a robust, profoundly questioning criticism of science within the scientific disciplines? One reason, I assume, is that such self-criticism, especially in public, would be considered "unprofessional." Another reason is that the modern sciences, working always in such proximity to "application," are simply too lucrative or too potentially lucrative to be self-critical. The professions increasingly have adopted the standards and thought patterns of business: If you're making money, what can be wrong? The criticism of science most familiar to ordinary citizens is more than likely to take the form of a public protest against some ruinous local manifestation of applied science. The most ubiquitous and unignorable result of modern chemistry, for example, is pollution, but typically this result is dealt with by ordinary citizens, not by chemists.

In 1959, C. P. Snow spoke of science as having an "automatic corrective" (*The Two Cultures,* Cambridge, 1998, p. 8). At that time, maybe, one could reasonably suppose that "pure" science, safely withdrawn from application, might by its own processes of experimentation and proof more or less automatically correct itself. By now we know that the applied sciences are subject to no such corrective. The scale of experimentation has become too greatly enlarged, for now science may be said to be conducting many of its experiments on the scale of the world. Among the results are Chernobyl, the ozone hole, the acceleration of species extinction, and universal pollution.

If there are critics of science in the governments and the bureaucracies, they are largely inaudible. In the universities, the scientists generally proceed from promotion to promotion and from grant to grant, leaving few recorded moments of conscience or professional self-doubt; and the professors of the humanities seem for the most part merely to be abashed by the sciences, deferring to their certainties, adopting their values, admiring their wealth, and longing even to imitate their methodology and their jargon. The journalists think it intellectually chic to stand open-mouthed before any wonder of science whatsoever. The media, cultivating their mediocrity, seem quite comfortably unaware that many of the calamities from which science is expected to save the world were caused in the first place by science—which meanwhile is busy propagating further calamities, hailed now as wonders, from which later it will undertake to save the world. Nobody, so far as I have heard, is attempting to figure out how much of the progress resulting from this enterprise is *net*. It is as if a whole population has been genetically deprived of the ability to subtract.

I know that there are some scientists who are speaking and writing sound criticism of science or of scientific abuses of science, but these people seem to have the status of dissidents or heretics; they are not accepted as partners in a necessary dialogue. Typically, their criticisms and objections are not even answered. (If you are making money and have power, why debate?) In short, the scientific critics of science are not effective. That there has been no effective criticism of science is demonstrated, for instance, by science's failure to attend to the possibility of small-scale or cheap or low-energy or ecologically benign technologies. Most applications of science to our problems result in large payments to large corporations and in damages to ecosystems and communities. These eventually will have to be subtracted (but not, if they can help it, by the inventors or manufacturers) from whatever has been gained.

LIFE IS A MIRACLE

III. On Edward O. Wilson's *Consilience*

APPARENTLY everywhere in the "developed world" human communities and their natural and cultural supports are being destroyed, not by natural calamities or "acts of God" or invasion by foreign enemies, but by a sort of legalized vandalism known as "the economy." The economy now famously depends upon the authority and the applicable knowledge of science. It would therefore be useful to say what is the character of this science that has benefited us in so many ways, and yet has cost us so dearly and exacted from us such deference and such questionable permissions.

Since I am not able to conduct any kind of survey, I will focus my study upon a single book: *Consilience,* by Edward O. Wilson. I am aware of the several objections to treating any one book as representative, but I am encouraged to do so, not only by the advantage of economy, but also by my belief that Mr. Wilson's assumptions are widely shared both by his colleagues and by non-scientists, and that there is no idea in his book that would be surprising to any fairly regular reader of articles on science in a daily newspaper. I think, in short, that despite his pretensions to iconoclasm, Mr. Wilson speaks for a popular scientific orthodoxy. His book reads as though it was written to confirm the popular belief that science is entirely good, that it leads to unlimited progress, and that it has (or will have) all the answers.

I am interested in Mr. Wilson's book also because, like me, he is a conservationist. We have perhaps some other things in common, but we have differences too, and these concern me just as much and (as will presently be evident) more seriously and at greater length. Our fundamental difference may be that he is a university man through and through, and I have always been most comfortable out of school. Whereas Mr. Wilson apparently is satisfied with the modern university's commitment to departmented specialization, professional standards, industry-sponsored research, and a scheme of promotion and tenure based upon publication, I am distrustful of that commitment and think it has done harm, both to learning and to the world.

Obviously, I have no authority from which to question Mr. Wilson's scientific knowledge, which I believe to be great and admirable, as human knowledge goes. My interest, rather, is in his attitudes toward what he knows and (more important) what he doesn't know. It is in these attitudes, I believe, that he is most conventional, and in them he most conforms to the values and the psychology of industrialism.

To show how Mr. Wilson stands on the issue of knowledge

and ignorance, I will catalogue here his fundamental biases and assumptions as they appear in his book, observing when he is being properly scientific, and when he is not. *Consilience* is in effect a scientific credo; its opinions are plainly stated.

1. Materialism

Mr. Wilson is, to begin with, a materialist. He believes that this is "a lawful material world" (p. 8), all the laws of which can be explained and understood empirically, and are subject to scientific proofs. He holds that "all tangible phenomena, from the birth of stars to the workings of social institutions, are based on material processes that are ultimately reducible . . . to the laws of physics" (p. 266).

Science is an enterprise of materiality, dealing in empirical proofs, in the tangible, the measurable, and the countable. And so, in terms of procedure, there can be no objection to Mr. Wilson's materialism; he is a scientist, and from a scientist we require truths that are materially verifiable. But as a doctrine of belief, materialism takes him into several kinds of trouble. These troubles show up pretty plainly against his obviously genuine concern for conservation of the natural world.

A minor problem, perhaps, is the tendency of materialism to objectify the world, dividing it from the "objective observer" who studies it. The world thus becomes "the environment," a word which Mr. Wilson uses repeatedly when speaking of conservation, and which means "surroundings," a place that one is *in* but not *of*. The question raised by this objectifying procedure and its vocabulary is whether the problems of conservation can be accurately defined by an objective observer who observes at an intellectual remove, forgetting that he eats, drinks, and breathes the so-called environment.

A more serious problem is this: A theoretical materialism so strictly principled as Mr. Wilson's is inescapably deterministic. We and our works and acts, he holds, are determined by our genes, which are determined by the laws of biology, which are determined ultimately by the laws of physics. He sees that this directly contradicts the idea of free will, which even as a scientist he seems unwilling to give up, and which as a conservationist he cannot afford to give up. He deals with this dilemma oddly and inconsistently.

First, he says that we have, and need, "the illusion of free will" (p. 119) which, he says further, is "biologically adaptive" (p. 120). I have read his sentences several times, hoping to find that I have misunderstood them, but I am afraid that I understand them. He is saying that there is an evolutionary advantage in illusion. The proposition that our ancestors survived because they were foolish enough to believe an illusion is certainly optimistic, but it does not seem very probable. And what are we to think of a materialism that can be used to validate an illusion? Mr. Wilson nevertheless insists upon his point; in another place he speaks of "self-deception" as granting to our species the "adaptive edge" (p. 97).

Later, in discussing the need for conservation, Mr. Wilson affirms the Enlightenment belief that we can "choose wisely" (p. 297). How a wise choice can be made on the basis of an illusory freedom of will is impossible to conceive, and Mr. Wilson wisely chooses not to try to conceive it.

2. Materialism and Mystery

Furthermore, as internally awry and inconsistent as it is, Mr. Wilson makes of his materialism a little platform from which to look down upon (as he thinks) and patronize the opposition. He is a *militant* materialist, with a doctrinaire intolerance for any sort of mystery—or, for that matter, any sort of ambiguity or uncertainty. He understands mystery as attributable entirely to human ignorance, and thereby appropriates it for the future of human science; in his formula, the unknown = the to-be-known. I will have more to say about this presently. For now, it is enough merely to notice that he has no ability to confront mystery (or even the unknown) as such, and therefore has learned none of the lessons that humans have always learned when they have confronted mystery as such. His book is an exercise in a sort of academic hubris.

If modern science is a religion, then one of its presiding deities must be Sherlock Holmes. To the modern scientist as to the great detective, every mystery is a problem, and every problem can be solved. A mystery can exist only because of human ignorance, and human ignorance is always remediable. The appropriate response is not deference or respect, let alone reverence, but pursuit of "the answer."

This pursuit, however, is properly scientific only so long as the mystery is empirically or rationally solvable. When a scientist denies or belittles a mystery that cannot be solved, then he or she is no longer within the bounds of science.

Thus, when Mr. Wilson asserts that *Paradise Lost* owes nothing to "God's guidance of Milton's thoughts, as the poet himself believed" (p. 213), he is talking far beyond the reach of proof. He does not consider that *Paradise Lost* is the poem it is because Milton was a man faithful and humble enough to invoke the assistance of the "Heav'nly Muse." The only empirical truth available here is that Milton, believing, wrote *Paradise Lost,* and that Mr. Wilson, disbelieving, wrote *Consilience,* a book of a different order.

Believing that whatever is intangible does not exist, Mr. Wilson like many materialists, atheists, rationalists, realists, etc., thinks he has struck a killing blow against religious faith when he has asked to see its evidence. But of course religious faith *begins* with the discovery that there is no "evidence." There is no argument or trail of evidence or course of experimentation that can connect unbelief and belief.

By insisting upon so narrow a definition of reality, Mr. Wilson does not defeat religion, but only misunderstands it. He does not appreciate, because he cannot suspect, the possibility that religious faith may be a way of knowing things that cannot otherwise be known. Misunderstanding religion, he often appropriates and misuses such words as *transcendent, create, archetype, reverence,* and *sacred.*

In his chapter on "Ethics and Religion," he has "constructed a debate" between "the transcendentalist" (a straw man) and "the empiricist" (a stuffed shirt). The empiricist, having found the transcendentalist's simple-minded argument (rigged for defeat by Mr. Wilson) to be lacking in "objective evidence" and "statistical proofs," then proceeds to make the same sort of irrational swerve that Mr. Wilson himself made previously in affirming "the illusion of free will." Empiricism, the empiricist concedes, "is bloodless. People need . . . the poetry of affirmation. . . . It would be a sorry day if we abandoned our venerated sacral traditions. It would be a tragic misreading of history to expunge *under God* from the American Pledge of Allegiance. Whether atheists or true believers, let oaths be taken with hand on the Bible. . . . Call upon priests and ministers and rabbis to bless civil ceremony with prayer . . ." All this, Mr. Wilson calls "the presence of poetry" (p. 247).

"But to share reverence," the empiricist continues hopefully, "is not to surrender the precious self . . ." (p. 248). A language can hardly endure this sort of abuse. It is impossible to tell what Mr. Wilson may mean by "share reverence," but to *feel* reverence, to *be* reverent, is exactly to surrender the "precious self," and is nothing else.

And then the empiricist administers his coup de grâce: "We can be proud as a species because, having discovered that we are alone, we owe the gods very little" (p. 248). This would be a noble blasphemy, like that of Job's wife, if the empiricist or Mr. Wilson believed in the gods, but neither one of them does. It is only a weary little cliché of a too familiar "scientific" iconoclasm—hubris without a bang.

But this materialism raises a question that *Consilience* does not acknowledge. If at last "all tangible phenomena" are empirically reduced to the laws of physics, then we will merely have completed a circle. We will have arrived again at the question that preceded Genesis: Where did the physical world come from? And physics of course can have no answer.

The principal point to be made, so far, is that Mr. Wilson's initially reputable materialism has led him far beyond objective evidence and statistical proofs and into what looks very much like poppycock. More examples will follow.

3. Imperialism

Mr. Wilson's scientific "faith" (as he sometimes calls it) is in the ultimate empirical explainability of everything—that is, the "consilience" of all the disciplines "by the linking of facts and fact-based theory . . . to create a common groundwork of explanation" (p. 8). He concedes from time to time that he may be wrong, but this doubt is a mere gesture, entirely absent from the passages in which he is elatedly confident that he is right. His humility is only etiquette, not a conviction or even an attitude. It is not involved in his thought, and his thought is unaffected by it. His book contains, moreover, several passages in which he writes with candor of the great difficulties and perhaps the impossibilities of the consilience he wishes for, but these also do not dampen or qualify his passionate conviction. Waving aside ignorance and mystery and human limitation as merely illusory or irrelevant, he claims not only all knowledge but all future knowledge and everything unknown as the property of science. So confident is he in his power to know that his book abounds in one-sentence definitions of, for examples, the mind, consciousness, meaning, mood, creativity, insanity, art, science, the self (all of these are in one chapter, "The Mind"). The definitions themselves are mostly jargon, singularly unhelpful—"What we call *meaning* is the linkage among the neural networks created by the spreading excitation that enlarges imagery and engages emotion" (p. 115)—but their purpose is clear enough: It is to take possession of the subject in the name of the idea of consilience.

This idea is explicitly imperialistic, and it is implicitly tyrannical. Mr. Wilson is perfectly frank about his territorial ambitions. He wishes to see all the disciplines linked or unified—but strictly on the basis of science. Non-scientists are not invited to the negotiations, or at least they are not to participate on their own terms: "The key to the exchange between [science and the arts] is ... reinvigoration of interpretation with the knowledge of science and its proprietary sense of the future" (p. 211). And if you have any doubt of the political and economic implications of modern science and of Mr. Wilson's advocacy, consider the following: "Governmental and private patrons of the brain scientists, like royal geographic commissions of past centuries, are generous. They know that history can be made by a single sighting of coastland, where inland lies virgin land and the future lineaments of empire" (p. 100).

Mr. Wilson's book scarcely acknowledges the existence of politics, and perhaps for good reason, for the putative ability to explain everything along with the denial of religion (or the appropriation of its appearances) is a property of political tyranny. So is the belief that one's explanations will save the world from some great threat. And Mr. Wilson himself, in his conviction that everything that is not a science *ought* to be and *will* be, shows himself to be a man with a fiercely proprietary mind and dire intentions toward the unenlightened.

The logic of his position is clear, and it is most disquieting. Would not, for example, any social theory be almost inescapably totalitarian if it were to be (in Mr. Wilson's terms) general, consilient, and predictive? Or if it *thought* it was, for the supposition would be just as dangerous to freedom as the fact. To suppose that the theory was predictive would prepare the way for a bloody "exogenous shock" (p. 201) that it did not predict. Mr. Wilson, in fact, alludes briefly to such possibilities in his chapter "The Enlightenment," but he does not confront the issue; he races past it and within three pages he is praising the Enlightenment's "new freedom": "It waved aside everything, every form of religious and civil authority, every imaginable fear, to give precedence to the ethic of free inquiry" (p. 37). The direction of Mr. Wilson's consilience, prescribed and announced, is toward an empirical dogma of dead certainty, "a common groundwork of explanation," the terms of which would exclude whatever cannot be empirically explained. Mere "humanitarianism" would do the rest: If you know with certainty what is true, should you not *enforce* the truth? If you see your poor subjects struggling and suffering in their error, how can you rightly forbear to impose the necessary corrections? Having spied out the coast, why should you not extend inland the "lineaments of empire"?

And this, though with some of us it would not be all right, would be incontestable if we had good reason to believe that everything could be explained on the terms proposed, which fortunately we do not. The only science we have or can have is *human* science; it has human limits and is involved always with human ignorance and human error. It is a fact that the solutions invented or discovered by science have tended to lead to new problems or to become problems themselves. Scientists discovered how to use nuclear energy to solve some problems, but any use of it is enormously dangerous to us all, and scientists have not discovered what to do with the waste. (They have not discovered what to do with old tires.) The availability of antibiotics leads to the overuse of antibiotics. And so on. Our daily lives are a daily mockery of our scientific pretensions. We are learning to know precisely the location of our genes, but significant numbers of us don't know the whereabouts of our children. Science does not seem to be lighting the way; we seem rather to be leapfrogging into the dark along series of scientific solutions, which become problems, which call for further solutions, which science is always eager to supply, and which it sometimes cannot supply. Sometimes it fails us infamously and fearfully. The so-called Y2K problem—the failure to manufacture computers capable of recognizing the year 2000—could have been prevented by perfectly ordinary human foresight, as limited as that is. The coming of the year 2000 could have been foretold by every child old enough to count. But among all the scientists who helped to develop "computer science," all who taught it in great universities, all who used it in their work, all who evangelized it as the answer to every intellectual problem, apparently no one with authority foresaw the Y2K fiasco until almost too late.

For a long time we humans have fairly successfully (but not invariably) avoided error within our systems of thought, but the systems themselves have often proved to be wrong. That is, our systems have made it possible (within the limits of the systems) to be consistent, but they have not preserved us from error. Our experience suggests that they cannot preserve us from error. Should we regret this? Probably not, since it is always the errors of our systems that have released us (so far) from the tyranny of our systems.

The presently dominant system of thought—which we should call, not "science," but "science-technology-and-industry"—has produced an unsurprising number of errors and an unsurprising number of failures. It is hard to see how our systems of thought could be other than fallible, once we grant that they cannot be contrived except by fallible creatures; fallibility is an infection in us that we inevitably communicate to our works. Who does not know this? Most of us begin every day with some kind of plan, and every day we see that plan altered or foiled because it necessarily lacks the scope of our nature and character, let alone that of reality. Our view of the world and even of our own experience is always to some degree distorted, oversimplified, or reduced, and so is varyingly liable to be in error. That we are in error means that our plans or systems tend to suffer the interference of bad surprises — and, let us not forget, also of good surprises. It is impossible to argue that we can know empirically anything that is beyond our mental capacity. What we understand has necessarily been limited by the limits of our understanding. Mr. Wilson predicts approvingly that "The world henceforth will be run by synthesizers, people able to put together the right information at the right time, think critically about it, and make important choices wisely" (p. 269). Synthesis, he says, is "holism." He does not acknowledge that the synthesis he is talking about will be neither whole nor holy, but rather an artifact made of parts that we have isolated and in our fashion understood ("We murder to dissect") and put together again in a way we understand.

The fallibility of a human system of thought is always the result of incompleteness. In order to include some things, we invariably exclude others. We can't include everything because we don't know everything; we can't comprehend what comprehends us. The incompleteness of a system is rarely if ever perceptible to those who made it or to those who benefit from it. To those who are excluded from it, the incompleteness of a system is, or eventually becomes, plain enough. One weakness of the present system, which Mr. Wilson does not mind, is that it excludes all inscrutable and ineffable things, including the life history of the human soul.

Another weakness, which Mr. Wilson does mind, is that it excludes the principle or the standard of ecological health. Science-technology-and-industry has enabled us to be precise (apparently) in describing objects that are extremely small and near or extremely large and far away. It has failed utterly to provide us with even adequate descriptions of the places and communities we live in—probably because it *cannot* do so. There are scientists, one must suppose, who know all about atoms or molecules or genes, or galaxies or planets or stars, but who do not know where they are geographically, historically, or ecologically. Our schools are turning out millions of graduates who do not know, in this sense, where they are. Certain lamentable results predictably follow. Mr. Wilson thinks the present system can correct itself merely by enlarging its present claims. I think the present system can correct itself only by conscientiously trying to include what it has so far excluded—which, of course, would make it an entirely different system with entirely different claims.

If one has a science that is manifestly incomplete—that is surrounded by mystery—and yet one believes with passionate intensity that it should, can, and will complete itself by means of a consilience of all the disciplines, then as an immediate and necessary effect one subjects one's language to a heavy strain. Mr. Wilson's project calls for a language of great assurance, but he is writing inescapably about what he does not know, and so his language often is necessarily tentative. The future that his thesis forces him to try to see into is finally as obscure to him as it is to the rest of us. His writing about consilience is always under the sway of conditional verbs, of protestations of faith, of "if" and "until" and "likely" and "perhaps." And so it is not scientific; it is not theorizing; it is only a fairly ordinary kind of human supposing, guided only by certain popular and professional prejudices.

But the most unscientific and the most disturbing thing about this book is Mr. Wilson's appropriation of whatever is unknown. He does this by variations on the themes of "until" or "not yet." He cannot bring himself to say that scientists do not know something; he must say that they do not know it *yet;* he must say that one thing cannot be known *until* another thing is known. He says repeatedly things like this: "The belief in the possibility of consilience beyond science and across the great branches of learning is not yet science. . . . It cannot be proved with logic from first principles or grounded in any definitive set of empirical tests, at least not by any yet conceived" (p. 9). This "not yet" forthrightly appropriates mystery as future knowledge. It takes possession of life and the future of life in the names of its would-be explainers—and, it follows, of its would-be exploiters. As soon as a mystery is scheduled for solution, it is no longer a mystery; it is a problem. The most tyrannic of all reductions has thus been accomplished; a self-aggrandizing science has thus asserted its "proprietary sense of the future."

The practical result of such language is a sort of moral blindness. We cannot derive sound thinking about propriety of scale and conduct from the proposition that what we need to know we do not know "yet." Such an idea simply overrides the issue of limits. Without a lively recognition of our own limits—chiefly of our knowledge and of our ability to know—we cannot even approach the issue of the limits of nature.

What is the possibility of "consilience beyond science and across the great branches of learning"?

We don't know yet.

Why do the innocent suffer?

We don't know yet.

*

I am not proposing, of course, that mental work of any sort can do without hypothesis or theory or any other way of articulating one's sense of possibility. Because our knowledge is discontinuous and we are ignorant of the future, we must grant the necessity of some manner of supposing from one point of evidence to another. At the same time it seems only fair to insist that this process should not be extended indefinitely without evidence, and that the points of evidence ought to be reasonably close together. In shallow water one may not risk much by postulating the existence of an as yet invisible stepping stone just beneath the surface. But if the water is deep and swift, one should not start across if some of the stepping stones are hypothetical. It is absurd to accumulate enormous quantities of nuclear waste, telling ourselves that we don't know *yet* how to dispose of it. We might face the future a good deal more confidently now if nuclear scientists had had the humility and the candor to say simply, We don't know.

Clearly, there ought to be a limit beyond which we cease to hedge our ignorance with promises to "continue to study the problem." Scrupulous minds, in this age as in any other, not only must be constrained occasionally to confess ignorance, but also must continue to live with the old proposition that some things are not knowable. *Consilience,* at any rate, shows us a man's mind leaping with exuberant confidence from one merely conjectural stepping stone to another, oblivious of the rushing waters.

4. Reductionism

Reductionism, like materialism, has uses that are appropriate, and it also can be used inappropriately. It is appropriately used as a way (one way) of understanding what is empirically known or empirically knowable. When it becomes merely an intellectual "position" confronting what is not empirically known or knowable, then it becomes very quickly absurd, and also grossly desensitizing and false. Like materialism, reductionism belongs legitimately to science; as an article of belief, it causes trouble.

According to Mr. Wilson, "Science . . . is the *organized, systematic enterprise that gathers knowledge about the world and condenses the knowledge into testable laws and principles"* [his italics] (p. 53). He says further that "The cutting edge of science is reductionism, the breaking apart of nature into its natural constituents" (p. 54). And reductionism has "a deeper agenda," which is "to fold the laws and principles of each level of organization into those at more general, hence more fundamental levels. Its strong form is total consilience, which holds that nature is organized by simple universal laws of physics to which all other laws and principles can eventually be reduced" (p. 55). Toward the end of his book, Mr. Wilson adds the following: "There is abundant evidence to support and none absolutely to refute the proposition that consilient explanations are congenial to the entirety of the great branches of learning" (p. 266).

Mr. Wilson's definitions of science and reductionism, granting him his prejudices, seem to me perfectly appropriate. His definition of consilience, however, like his exposition of it, becomes more contestable the farther it goes.

There obviously is a necessary usefulness in the processes of reduction. They are indispensable to scientists—and to the rest of us as well. It is valuable (sometimes) to know the parts of a thing and how they are joined together, to know what things do and do not have in common, and to know the laws or principles by which things cohere, live, and act. Such inquiries are native to human thought and work.

But reductionism also has one inherent limitation that is paramount, and that is abstraction: its tendency to allow the particular to be absorbed or obscured by the general. It is a curious paradox of science that its empirical knowledge of the material world gives rise to abstractions such as statistical averages which have no materiality and exist only as ideas. There is, empirically speaking, no average and no type. Between the species and the specimen the creature itself, the individual creature, is lost. Having been classified, dissected, and explained, the creature has disappeared into its class, anatomy, and explanation. The tendency is to equate the creature (or its habitat) with one's formalized knowledge of it. Mr.

Wilson is somewhat aware of this problem for he insists upon the importance of "synthesis and integration" (p. 54). But he does not acknowledge that synthesis and integration are merely parts of an explanation, which is invariably and inevitably less than the thing explained. The synthesizing and integrating scientist is only ordering and making sense of as much as he knows. He is not making whole that which he has taken apart, and he should not claim credit for putting together what was already together.

The uniqueness of an individual creature is inherent, not in its physical or behavioral anomalies, but in its *life*. Its life is not its "life history," the typical cycle of members of its species from conception to reproduction to death. Its life is all that happens to it in its place. Its wholeness is inherent in its life, not in its physiology or biology. This wholeness of creatures and places together is never going to be apparent to an intelligence coldly determined to be empirical or objective. It shows itself to affection and familiarity.

The frequent insultingness of modern (scientific-technological-industrial) medicine is precisely its inclination to regard individual patients apart from their lives, as representatives or specimens of their age, sex, pathology, economic status, or some other category. The specialist to whom you have been "referred" may never have seen you before, may know nothing about you, and may never see you again, and yet he or she presumes to know exactly what is wrong with you. The same insultingness is now also a commonplace of politics, which treats individuals as representatives of racial, sexual, geographic, economic, ideological, and other categories, each with typical faults, complaints, rights, or virtues.

Science speaks properly a language of abstraction and abstract categories when it is properly trying to sort out and put in order the things it knows. But it often assumes improperly that it has said—or known—enough when it has spoken of "the cell" or "the organism," "the genome" or "the ecosystem" and given the correct scientific classification and name. Carried too far, this is a language of false specification and pretentious exactitude, never escaping either abstraction or the cold-heartedness of abstraction.

The giveaway is that even scientists do not speak of their loved ones in categorical terms as "a woman," "a man," "a child," or "a case." Affection requires us to break out of the abstractions, the categories, and confront the creature itself in its life in its place. The importance of this for Mr. Wilson's (and my) cause of conservation can hardly be overstated. For things cannot survive as categories but only as individual creatures living uniquely where they live.

We know enough of our own history by now to be aware that people *exploit* what they have merely concluded to be of value, but they *defend* what they love. To defend what we love we need a particularizing language, for we love what we particularly know. The abstract, "objective," impersonal, dispassionate language of science can, in fact, help us to know certain things, and to know some things with certainty. It can help us, for instance, to know the value of species and of species diversity. But it cannot replace, and it cannot become, the language of familiarity, reverence, and affection by which things of value ultimately are protected.

The abstractions of science are too readily assimilable to the abstractions of industry and commerce, which see everything as interchangeable with or replaceable by something else. There is a kind of egalitarianism which holds that any two things equal in price are equal in value, and that nothing is better than anything that may profitably or fashionably replace it. Forest = field = parking lot; if the price of alteration is right, then there is no point in quibbling over differences. One place is as good as another, one use is as good as another, one life is as good as another—if the price is right. Thus political sentimentality metamorphoses into commercial indifference or aggression. This is the industrial doctrine of the interchangeability of parts, and we apply it to places, to creatures, and to our fellow humans as if it were the law of the world, using all the while a sort of middling language, imitated from the sciences, that cannot speak of heaven or earth, but only of concepts. This is a rhetoric of nowhere, which forbids a passionate interest in, let alone a love of, anything in particular.

Directly opposed to this reduction or abstraction of things is the idea of the preciousness of individual lives and places. This does not come from science, but from our cultural and religious traditions. It is not derived, and it is not derivable, from any notion of egalitarianism. If all are equal, none can be precious. (And perhaps it is necessary to stop here to say that this ancient delight in the individuality of creatures is not the same thing as what we now mean by "individualism." It is the opposite. Individualism, in present practice, refers to the supposed "right" of an individual to act alone, in disregard of other individuals.)

We now have the phenomenon of "mitigation banking" by which a developer may purchase the "right" to spoil one place by preserving another. Science can measure and balance acreages in this way just as cold-heartedly as commerce; developers involved in such trading undoubtedly have the assistance of ecologists.

Nothing insists that one place is not interchangeable with another except affection. If the people who live in such places and love them cannot protect them, nobody can.

It is not quite imaginable that people will exert themselves greatly to defend creatures and places that they have dispassionately studied. It is altogether imaginable that they will greatly exert themselves to defend creatures and places that they have involved in their lives and invested their lives in—and of course I know that many scientists make this sort of commitment.

*

I have been working this morning in front of a window where I have been at work on many mornings for thirty-seven years. Though I have been busy, today as always I have been aware of what has been happening beyond the window. The ground is whitened by patches of melting snow. The river, swollen with the runoff, is swift and muddy. I saw four wood ducks riding the current, apparently for fun. A great blue heron was fishing, standing in water up to his belly feathers. Through binoculars I saw him stoop forward, catch, and swallow a fish. At the feeder on the window sill, goldfinches, titmice, chickadees, nuthatches, and cardinals have been busy at a heap of free (to them) sunflower seeds. A flock of crows has found something newsworthy in the cornfield across the river. The woodpeckers are at work, and so are the squirrels. Sometimes from this outlook I have seen wonders: deer swimming across, wild turkeys feeding, a pair of newly fledged owls, otters at play, a coyote taking a stroll, a hummingbird feeding her young, a peregrine falcon eating a snake. When the trees are not in leaf, I can see the wooded slopes on both sides of the valley. I have known this place all my life. I long to protect it and the creatures who belong to it. During the thirty-seven years I have been at work here, I have been thinking a good part of the time about how to protect it. This is a small, fragile place, a slender strip of woodland between the river and the road. I know that in two hours a bulldozer could make it unrecognizable to me, and perfectly recognizable to every "developer."

The one thing that I know above all is that even to hope to protect it, I have got to break out of all the categories and confront it as it is; I must be present in its presence. I know at least some of the categories and value them and have found them useful. But here I am in my life, and I know I am not here as a representative white male American human, nor are the birds and animals and plants here as representatives of their sex or species. We all have our ways, forms, and habits. We all are what we are partly because we are here and not in another place. Some of us are mobile; some of us (such as the trees) have to be content merely to be flexible. All of us who are mobile are required by happenstance and circumstance and accident to make choices that are not instinctive, and that force us out of categories into our lives here and now. Even the trees are under this particularizing influence of place and time. Each one, responding to happenstance and circumstance and accident, has assumed a shape not quite like that of any other tree of its kind. The trees stand rooted in their mysteriously determined places, no place quite like any other, in strange finality. The birds and animals have their nests in holes and burrows and crotches, each one's place a little unlike any other in the world—and so is the nest my mate and I have made.

In all of the thirty-seven years I have worked here, I have been trying to learn a language particular enough to speak of this place as it is and of my being here as I am. My success, as I well know, has been poor enough, and yet I am glad of the effort, for it has helped me to make, and to remember always, the distinction between reduction and the thing reduced. I know the usefulness of reductive language. To know that I am "a white male American human," that a red bird with black wings is "a scarlet tanager," that a tree with white bark is "a sycamore," that this is "a riparian plant community"—all that is helpful to a necessary kind of thought. But when I try to make my language more particular, I see that the life of this place is always emerging beyond expectation or prediction or typicality, that it is unique, given to the world minute by minute, only once, never to be repeated. And then is when I see that this life is a miracle, absolutely worth having, absolutely worth saving.

We are alive within mystery, by miracle. "Life," wrote Erwin Chargaff, "is the continual intervention of the inexplicable" (*Heraclitean Fire,* The Rockefeller University Press, 1978, p. 20). We have more than we can know. We know more than we can say. The constructions of language (which is to say the constructions of thought) are formed *within* experience, not the other way around. Finally we live beyond words, as also we live beyond computation and beyond theory. There is no reason whatever to assume that the languages of science are less limited than other languages. Perhaps we should wish that after the processes of reduction, scientists would return, not to the processes of synthesis and integration, but to the world of our creatureliness and affection, our joy and grief, that precedes and (so far) survives all of our processes.

5. Creatures as Machines

There is a reduction, by now more formulaic than procedural, that seems endemic to modern science, and from science it has spread everywhere. I mean the definition or identification of the world and all its creatures as "machines." This is one of the fundamental assertions in *Consilience.* The Enlightenment thinkers, Mr. Wilson says, encouraged us to "think of the world as God's machine"— "if you still insist on a divine intervention" (p. 22). A little later he says, "People, after all, are just extremely complicated machines" (p. 30). Further on, he says that we are "organic machines" (p. 82), and that "an organism is a machine" (p. 91).

This machine business may once have had meaning. It may have been a way of asserting belief in the integrity of Creation and the physical coherence of creatures; it may have been a way of insisting on the indispensability of part to whole. The machine, in other words, had a certain usefulness as a *metaphor.* But the legitimacy of a metaphor depends upon our understanding of its limits. A friend of mine remembered an aunt who noted, correctly, that when Jesus said "I am the door," He did not mean that He had hinges and a knob. We must be careful to remember that a profession is not altogether like a field, or a camera altogether like a room, or a pedigree altogether like a crane's foot.

When a metaphor is construed as an equation, it is out of control; when it is construed as an identity, it is preposterous. If we are to assume that our language means anything at all, then the world is not a machine, and neither is an organism. A machine, to state only the greatest and most obvious difference, is a human artifact, and a world or an organism is not.

But Mr. Wilson, like many others, is fond of this error, and he carries it further. He says, first, that "the brain is a machine" (p. 96), and then he says that "the mind . . . is the brain at work" (p. 98). To lock the subject into this definition, and so forestall any difference of opinion or the introduction of any contradictory evidence, he says, "The surest way to grasp complexity in the brain, as in any other biological system, is to think of it as an engineering problem" (p. 102).

*

The proposed theory of human mentality, then, is a simple formula: mind = brain = machine. That is to say that the mind is singular, material, and altogether what it is in itself—just as a machine (once made) is a machine per se, singular and material. This is pretty close to what I would call the Tarzan theory of the mind, invented by Edgar Rice Burroughs. The Tarzan theory holds that a human, raised entirely by apes, would have a mind nonetheless fully human: a human brain, in (so to speak) a social and cultural vacuum, would still function on its own as a human mind.

But this raises an interesting question: Is there such a thing as a mind which is merely a brain which is a machine? Would one have a mind if one had no body, or no body except for a brain (whether or not it is a machine)—if one had no sense organs, no hands, no ability to move or speak, no sensory pains or pleasures, no appetites, no bodily needs? If we grant (for the sake of argument) that such may be theoretically possible, we must concede at the same time that it is not imaginable, and for the most literal of reasons: Such a mind could contain no image.

And now let us grant the mind a body and all that the body

brings with it and implies: sense, imagery, motion, desire. Another question arises: Would such a mind alone be a mind? Would one mind alone, alone and therefore lacking a language and any need for signs or signification, be recognizable as a mind? Again, we may grant that this is theoretically possible (though I see no reason why we should). But if we encountered such a mind, how would we know that it was a mind?

Suppose, then, that we put two embodied minds together, making them male and female, and yet deny them a habitat and any familiarity of place and time. Now we would be approaching something recognizably a mind, because we would have two. There would need to be some sort of language. These two minds would be different, they would have desires toward one another, they would need to negotiate. But without a dwelling place this language would be too poverty-stricken and crude to be called human. We can grant, as before, a theoretical possibility to this sort of mind, at the same time being forced to grant also that it would not be recognizably a human mind. (All of us have seen, and most of us have been, adolescent lovers who had nothing to talk about but themselves, and we know how intelligent *that* is.)

But we have been begging the question all along with our grantings of theoretical possibility, for one can't be a brain without a body, or a body (for very long) without a familiar homeland. To have one mind you have got to have at least two (and undoubtedly many more) and a world. We could call this the Adam and Eve theory of the mind. The correct formula, in fact, is more like this: mind = brain + body + world + local dwelling place + community + history. "History" here would mean not just documented events but the whole heritage of culture, language, memory, tools, and skills. Mind in this definition has become hard to locate in an organ, organism, or place. It has become an immaterial presence or possibility that is capable of being embodied and placed.

And here the difference between organisms and machines becomes clearer. The idea of a mind and the idea of an organism are not separate ideas. Or we could say that they are momentarily separable—but only momentarily—for the purposes of thought. Every living creature embodies enough mind to know how to be itself and survive in its place, else it cannot live. A machine embodies none of the mind that made it, and it has nothing of an organism's dependence on its world and community and place and history. A machine, if shot into outer space never to return, would simply go on and on being a machine; after it ran out of fuel or traveled beyond guidance, it would still be a machine. A human mind, necessarily embodied, if shot into outer space never to return, would die as soon as it went beyond its sustaining connections and references.

How far from home can a mind go and still be a mind? Probably no scientist has yet made this measurement, but we can answer confidently: Not too far. How far can a machine go from home (supposing, for the sake of argument, that a machine has a home) and still be a machine? Theoretically, if it is not destroyed, it can go on forever.

If the mind is incomplete without a home, without familiar associations and points of reference outside itself, then it becomes possible to argue that the longer the mind of an individual or a community is at home the better it may become. But this "better" implies the willingness and the ability to practice the virtues of domestic economy: frugality, continuous household maintenance and repair, neighborliness, good husbandry of soil and water, ecosystem and watershed.

If the mind fails in this earthly housekeeping, it can only get worse. How much can a mind diminish its culture, its community and its geography—how much topsoil, how many species can it lose—and still be a mind?

*

If the mind is as complexly formed as I have suggested, then it seems unlikely that the mind of an individual can be the origin of intelligence or truth, any more than an individual brain can be. And I fail to see how an individual brain alone can have any originating power whatsoever.

Of the material origin of intelligence or truth, or even of mind, any answer given will lead only to another question. To settle the matter, one would have to *see* experimentally the point at which some physical activity or excitement of the brain, alone, transformed itself into an original idea.

But how can an idea, which is not material, have a material origin? "Average," for example, is an idea which partakes of none of the physical properties of the things that are averaged. Materialism itself is an idea, just as immaterial as any other. And Edward O. Wilson, despite his materialism, shows himself to be a man as interested in ideas as in the material world.

If ideas are not material, how can they have a material origin? If they are not material in origin, how can their origin be explained by materialist science? This is the major fault line of Mr. Wilson's book: His interest in explaining the origin of things whose authentic existence is denied by the terms of the proposed investigation.

*

Anybody who thinks that this "scientific" reduction of creatures to machines is merely an issue to be pondered by academic intellectuals is in need of a second thought. I suppose that there are no religious implications in this reductionism, for if you think creatures are machines, you have no religion. For artists who do not think of themselves as machines, there is one artistic implication: Don't be mechanical. But the implications for politics and conservation are profound.

It is evident to us all by now that modern totalitarian governments become more mechanical as they become more total. Under *any* political system there is always a tendency to expect the government to work with mechanical "efficiency"—that is, with speed and no redundancy. (Mechanical efficiency always "externalizes" inefficiencies, such as exhaust fumes, but still one can understand the temptation.) Our system, however, which claims freedom as its purpose, involves several powerful concepts that tend to retard the speed and efficiency of government and to make it unmechanical: the ideas of government by consent of the governed, of minority rights, of checks and balances, of trial by jury, of appellate courts, and so on. If we were to implement politically the idea that creatures are machines, we would lose all of those precious impediments to mechanical efficiency in government. The basis of our rights and liberties would be undermined. If people are machines, what is wrong, for example, with slavery? Why should a machine wish to be free? Why should a large machine honor a small machine's quaint protestations that it has thoughts or feelings or affections or aspirations?

It is not beside the point to remember that our government at times has seen fit to look upon the prosperity of many small producers and manufacturers as a political and economic good, and so has placed appropriate restraints upon the mechanical efficiencies of monopolists and foreign competitors. It is not mechanically efficient to recognize that unrestrained competition between an individual farmer or storekeeper and a great corporation is neither democratic nor fair. I suppose that our so-called conservatives have at least no inconsistency to apologize for; they have espoused the "freedom" of the corporations and their "global economy," and they have no conflicting inhibitions in favor of democracy and fairness. The "liberals," on the other hand, have made political correctness the measure of their social policy at the same time that they advance the economic determinism of the conservatives. Reconciling these "positions" is not rationally possible; you cannot preserve the traditional rights and liberties of a democracy by the mechanical principles of economic totalitarianism.

But for the time being (may it be short) the corporations thrive, and they are doing so at the expense of everything else. Their dogma of the survival of the wealthiest (i.e. mechanical efficiency) is the dominant intellectual fashion. A letter to the *New York Times* of July 8, 1999 stated it perfectly: "While change is difficult for those affected, the larger, more efficient business organization will eventually emerge and industry consolidation will occur to the benefit of the many." When you read or hear those words "larger" and "more efficient" you may expect soon to encounter the word "inevitable," and this letter writer conformed exactly to the rule: "We should not try to prevent the inevitable consolidation of the farming industry." This way of talking is now commonplace among supposedly intelligent people, and it has only one motive: the avoidance of difficult thought. Or one might as well say that the motive is the avoidance of thought, for that use of the word "inevitable" obviates the need to consider any alternative, and a person confronting only a single possibility is well beyond any need to think. The message is: "The machine is coming. If you are small and in the way, you must lie down and be run over." So high a level of mental activity is readily achieved by terrapins.

*

The reduction of creatures to machines is in principle directly opposed to the effort of conservation. It is, in the first place, part and parcel of the determinism that derives from materialism. Conservation depends upon our ability to make qualitative choices affecting our influence on the ecosystems we live in or from. Machines can make no such choices, and neither, presumably, can creatures who are machines. If we are machines, we can only do as we are bidden to do by the mechanical laws of our mechanical nature. By what determinism we *regret* our involvement in our mechanical devastations of the natural world has not been explained by Mr. Wilson or (so far as I know) by anybody.

But suppose we *don't* subscribe to this determinism. Suppose we don't believe that creatures are machines. Then we must see the extent to which conservation has been hampered by this idea, whether consciously advocated by scientists or thoughtlessly mouthed about in the media and in classrooms. The widespread belief that creatures *are* machines obviously makes it difficult to form an advocacy for creatures *against* machines. To confuse or conflate creatures with machines not only makes it impossible to see the differences between them; it also masks the conflict between creatures and machines that under industrialism has resulted so far in an almost continuous sequence of victories of machines over creatures.

To say as much puts me on difficult ground, I know. To confess, these days, that you think some things are more important than machines is almost sure to bring you face to face with somebody who will accuse you of being "against technology"—against, that is, "the larger, more efficient business organization" that will emerge inevitably "to the benefit of the many."

And so I would like to be as plain as possible. What I am against—and without a minute's hesitation or apology—is our slovenly willingness to allow machines and the idea of the machine to prescribe the terms and conditions of the lives of creatures, which we have allowed increasingly for the last two centuries, and are still allowing, at an incalculable cost to other creatures *and to ourselves.* If we state the problem that way, then we can see that the way to correct our error, and so deliver ourselves from our own destructiveness, is to quit using our technological capability as the reference point and standard of our economic life. We will instead have to measure our economy by the health of the ecosystems and human communities where we do our work.

It is easy for me to imagine that the next great division of the world will be between people who wish to live as creatures and people who wish to live as machines.

6. Originality and the "Two Cultures"

If one of the deities or mythological prototypes of modern science is Sherlock Holmes, another, surely, is the pioneering navigator or land discoverer: Christopher Columbus or Daniel Boone. Mr. Wilson's book returns to this image again and again. He says that "Original discovery is everything" (p. 56). And he speaks of "new terrain" (p. 12), "the frontier" (pp. 39 and 56), "the mother lode" and "virgin soil" (p. 56), "the growing edge" (p. 39) and "the cutting edge" (pp. 99 and 201), and "virgin land" (p. 100). He speaks of scientists as "prospectors" (pp. 38 and 56), as navigators who "steer for blue water, abandoning sight of land for a while" (p. 58), and (in several places) as explorers of unmapped territory.

This figure of the heroic discoverer, so prominent in the mind of so eminent a scientist, dominates as well the languages of scientific journalism and propaganda. It defines, one guesses, the ambition or secret hope of most scientists, industrial technologists, and product developers: to go where nobody has previously gone, to do what nobody has ever done.

There is nothing intrinsically wrong with heroic discovery. However, it is as much subject to criticism as anything else. That is to say that it may be either good or bad, depending on what is discovered and what use is made of it. Intelligence minimally requires us to consider the possibility that we might well have done without some discoveries, and that there might be two opinions from different perspectives about any given discovery—for example, the opinion of Cortés, and that of Montezuma. Perhaps intelligence requires us to consider even that some unexplored territory had better be treated as forbidden territory.

As a personal ambition, heroic discovery has obvious risks, even for the heroically gifted. The greatest risk is that one will trade one's life—all the ordinary satisfactions of homeland and family life—for the sake of a hope not ordinarily realizable. William Butler Yeats saw these possibilities as mutually exclusive and the choice between them as inescapable; he was wrong, I think, and yet he was undoubtedly right about the cost of choosing work over life:

> The intellect of man is forced to choose
> Perfection of the life, or of the work,
> And if it take the second must refuse
> A heavenly mansion, raging in the dark.
>
> When all that story's finished, what's the news?
> In luck or out the toil has left its mark:
> That old perplexity an empty purse,
> Or the day's vanity, the night's remorse.
> ("The Choice," *Collected Poems,* 1954, p. 242)

Mr. Wilson believes that the desire to seek out "virgin land and the future lineaments of empire" is "basic to human nature" (p. 100). Maybe so, but it seems more likely to be basic to the nature of only some humans, among whom have been some of the worst. Its cultural justification is to be found in works of romantic individualism and self-glorification such as Tennyson's "Ulysses," in which the hero (rehabilitated from Dante's *Inferno*) yearns toward "that untraveled world," and desires

> To follow knowledge like a sinking star
> Beyond the utmost bound of human thought.

Dante, as Tennyson did not say, found this Ulysses in Hell among the Evil Counsellors. And we, in making a cultural ideal of the same heroic ambition, see only the good that we believe is inevitably in it, forgetting how much it may partake of adolescent fantasy, adult megalomania, and intellectual snobbery, or how closely allied it is to our continuing history of imperialism and colonialism.

As a *norm* of expectation or ambition, then, heroic discovery is potentially ruinous, and maybe insane. It is one of the versions of our obsession with "getting to the top." Unlike the culture of the European Middle Ages, which honored the vocations of the learned teacher, the country parson, and the plowman as well as that of the knight, or the culture of Japan in the Edo period which ranked the farmer and the craftsman above the merchant, our own culture places an absolute premium upon various kinds of stardom. This degrades and impoverishes ordinary life, ordinary work, and ordinary experience. It depreciates and underpays the work of the primary producers of goods, and of the performers of all kinds of essential but unglamorous jobs and duties. The inevitable practical results are that most work is now poorly done; great cultural and natural resources are neglected, wasted, or abused; the land and its creatures are destroyed; and the citizenry is poorly taught, poorly governed, and poorly served.

Moreover, in education, to place so exclusive an emphasis upon "high achievement" is to lie to one's students. Versions of Mr. Wilson's "original discovery is everything" are now commonly handed out in public schools. The goal of education-as-job-training, which is now the dominant pedagogical idea, is a high professional salary. Young people are being told, "You can be anything you want to be." Every student is given to understand that he or she is being prepared for "leadership." All of this is a lie. Original discovery is *not* everything. You don't, for instance, have to be an original discoverer in order to be a good science teacher. A high professional salary is *not* everything. You *can't* be everything you want to be; nobody can. Everybody *can't* be a leader; not everybody even wants to be. And these lies are not innocent. They lead to disappointment. They lead good young people to think that if they have an ordinary job, if they work with their hands, if they are farmers or housewives or mechanics or carpenters, they are no good.

C. P. Snow, in his 1959 lecture "The Two Cultures," alluded to this problem. His comment occurs in a footnote, but it is nevertheless maybe the most troubling insight of his lecture. One consequence of industrialism, he said, "is that there are no people left, clever, competent and resigned to a humble job.... Postal services, railway services, are likely slowly to deteriorate just because the people who once ran them are now being educated for different things" (p. 104).

*

Snow's general argument was that in Britain and other countries of the West, the literary and scientific cultures had become separated by lack of common knowledge and a common language. His lecture, which I think was never first-rate, is still provocative and useful; it was controversial from the start, and the events of the last forty years certainly have imposed questions and qualifications upon it. But his point, if not his bias, is still valid. The "two cultures" remain divided; they are divided both between and within themselves; and this state of things is still regrettable.

Mr. Wilson appears to accept Snow's argument without qualification, since it justifies his own project for reuniting all the intellectual disciplines by means of consilience. But on this issue of the primacy of originality and innovation, of the cutting edge and the unmapped territory, the scientific and the literary cultures appear now to be pretty much in agreement. The two cultures don't exactly meet under this heading, but here at least they overlap.

This agreement is to a considerable extent the result of the absorption of all the disciplines into the organization (and the value system) of the modern, corporatized university, and of the literary culture's envy of the power, wealth, and prestige of the scientific culture within that organization. Given the present structure of incentives and rewards, it is perhaps only natural that non-sciences would aspire to become sciences, and that non-scientists would aspire to be, like scientists, heroes of original discovery (or at least of "the liberation of the human spirit"), scouting the frontiers of human knowledge or experience, wielding the cutting edge of some social science or some critical theory or some "revolutionary" art.

If there is an economy of the life of the mind—as I assume there has to be, for the life of the mind involves the distribution of limited amounts of time, energy, and attention — then that economy, like any other, subsists upon the making of critical choices. You can't think, read, research, study, learn, or teach everything. To choose one thing is to choose against many things. To know some things well is to know other things not so well, or not at all. Knowledge is always surrounded by ignorance. We are, moreover, differently talented and are called by different vocations. All this explains, and to some extent justifies, any system of specialization in work or study. One cannot sensibly choose against specialization because, if for no other reason, all of us by nature are to some degree specialized. There can be no objection in principle to organizing a university as a convocation of specialties and specialists; that is what a university is bound to be.

But some serious questions remain, the most serious of which I would put this way: Can this convocation of specialists, who have been "called together" to learn and teach, actually come together? In other words, can the convocation become a conversation? For that, the convocation would have to have a common purpose, a common standard, and a common language. It would have to understand itself as a part, for better or worse, of the surrounding community. For reasons both selfish and altruistic, it would have to make the good health of its community the primary purpose of all its work. If that were the avowed purpose, then all the members and branches of the university would have to converse with one another, and their various professional standards would have to submit to the one standard of the community's health.

This has not happened in our universities. The opposite, in fact, is happening. Unlike the English agriculturist, Sir Albert Howard, who moved from his specialty, mycology, to the "one great subject" of health, the modern university specialist moves ever away from health toward the utter departmentalization and disintegration of the life of the mind and of communities. The various specialties are moving ever outward from any center of interest or common ground, becoming ever farther apart, and ever more unintelligible to one another. Among the causes, I think, none is more prominent than the by now ubiquitous and nearly exclusive emphasis upon originality and innovation. This emphasis, operating within the "channels" of administration, affects in the most direct and practical ways all the lives within the university. It imposes the choice of work over life, exacting not only the personal costs spoken of in Yeats's poem, but very substantial costs to the community as well. And these are costs that can be accounted.

"Over the years," Mr. Wilson writes, "I have been presumptuous enough to counsel new Ph.D.'s in biology as follows: If you choose an academic career you will need forty hours a week to perform teaching and administrative duties, another twenty hours on top of that to conduct respectable research, and still another twenty hours to accomplish really important research" (pp. 55-56). Mr. Wilson is thus prescribing to the young a normative work week of eighty hours. Since he mentions no days off, let us assume that he is speaking of seven workdays of about 11½ hours each, lasting, say, from eight o'clock in the morning until 7:30 at night, or until eight at night if we allow half an hour for lunch. There are 168 hours in a seven-day week. Eighty from 168 leaves 88 hours. If the young Ph.D. sleeps eight hours a night, that takes another 56 hours, leaving 32 hours, or about 4½ hours per day. In that 4½ hours he or she must eat, keep clean, shop, do domestic chores, commute, read, care for his or her (unfortunate) children, etc. The time left over may presumably be used for amusement and for taking part in family and community life.

I suppose we ought to yield a certain admiration to such a dedicated life of work and sacrifice. It is certain that all of us have benefited from such effort on the part of some people. But it is just as certain that we have been damaged and are threatened by similar effort on the part of other people. In fact, most people can be driven to such an extent only by a kind of professional or careerist panic. Young Ph.D's or assistant professors find themselves in a man-made evolutionary crisis known in the universities as "publish or perish." To survive they must "produce," for the fundamental academic fact of life is that (as Mr. Wilson puts it) "a discovery does not exist until it is safely reviewed and in print" (p. 59). All "tenure track" professors in all universities, at least until tenure, are under life-or-death pressure to "find their way to a publishable conclusion" (p. 64). If a tree falls in the absence of a refereed journal or a foundation, does it make a sound? The answer, in the opinion of the imitation corporate executives who now run our universities, is no.

This academic Darwinism inflicts severe penalties both upon those who survive and upon those who perish. Both must submit to an absolute economic system which values their lives strictly according to their "productivity"—which is to say that they submit to a form of slavery. Both must submit, at least until tenure, to a university-prescribed regimen of life in which time = work = original discovery = career, thus assuring the ascendancy of professional standards in the minds of the young, and the eclipse of any standard of any other kind. The modern university thus enforces obedience, not to the academic ideal of learning and teaching what is true, as a community of teachers and scholars passing on to the young the knowledge of the old, but obedience rather to the industrial economic ideals of high productivity and constant innovation. The problem here is not that we should object to hard work and exacting study, which any school might appropriately expect, but that we certainly can find reason to object to turning schools into factories, and to making originality or innovation the exclusive goal and measure of so much effort. Mr. Wilson in his counsel to the young is, in fact, helping to perpetuate a system of education that conforms exactly to the demands of the economic system the effects of which, as a conservationist, he so much regrets. The "cutting edge" is not critical or radical or intellectually adventurous. The cutting edge of science is now fundamentally the same as the cutting edge of product development. The university emphasis upon productivity and innovation is inherently conventional and self-protective. It is part and parcel of the status quo. The goal is innovation but not difference. The system exists to prevent "academic freedom" from causing unhappy surprises to corporations, governments, or university administrators.

The present conformity between science and the industrial economy is virtually required by the costliness of the favored kinds of scientific research and the consequent dependence of scientists on patronage. Mr. Wilson writes that "Science, like art, and as always through history, follows patronage" (p. 93). Even I know of some scientists whose work did not "follow patronage," and there certainly have been artists whose work did not, but this statement seems generally true of modern science. And on page 157, Mr. Wilson elaborates; there is, he says, "a cardinal principle in the conduct of scientific research: Find a paradigm for which you can raise money and attack with every method of analysis at your disposal." This principle, in effect, makes the patron the prescriber of the work to be done. It would seem to eliminate the scientist as a person or community member who would judge whether or not the work *ought* to be done. It removes the scientist from the human and ecological circumstances in which the work will have its effect, and which should provide one of the standards by which the work is to be judged; the scientist is thus isolated, by this principle of following patronage, in a career with a budget. What this has to do with the vaunted aim of pursuing truth cannot be determined until one knows where the money comes from and what the donor expects. The donor will determine what truth (and how much) will be pursued, and how far, and to what effect. The scientist, having succeeded or failed with one paradigm, will then presumably be free to find another, and another patron.

The young Ph.D.'s who work eighty hours a week in a system devoted to "really important research" are not going to have time to know their community, let alone to wonder about the possible effects of their work upon its health. They are not going to have time to confront the problems invariably raised by innovation, or to perform the necessary criticism. Nor, in reality, will they have time to know their students very well, or to teach very well. If your educational system gives the preponderance of its rewards (promotions, salary increases, tenure, publication, prizes, grants) to "original discovery" and "really important research," then to the same extent it discourages teaching. It is simply a matter of fact that if teachers know that their careers and their livelihoods depend almost entirely on research, then most will steal time from teaching to give to research—exactly as any rational person would expect.

Teaching, anyhow, cannot do well under the cult of innovation. Devotion to the new enforces a devaluation and dismissal of the old, which is necessarily the subject of teaching. Even if its goal is innovation, science does not *consist* of innovation; it consists of what has been done, what is so far known, what has been thought— just like the so-called humanities. And here we meet a strange and difficult question that may be uniquely modern: Can the past be taught, can it even be known, by people who have no respect for it? If you believe in the absolute superiority of the new, can you learn and teach anything identifiable as old? Here, as before, Mr. Wilson speaks from an entirely conventional point of view. He takes seriously no history before the Enlightenment, which he believes began the era of modern science. Of "prescientific cultures" he makes short work: "they are wrong, always wrong." They know nothing about "the real world," but can only "invent ingenious speculations and myths." And: "Without the instruments and accumulated knowledge of the natural sciences—physics, chemistry, and biology—humans are trapped in a cognitive prison. They are like intelligent fish born in a deep, shadowed pool" (p. 45). I think (or, anyhow, hope) he does not realize how merciless this is—for he has thus flipped away most human history, most human lives, and most of the human cultural inheritance—or how small and dull a world it leaves him in. To escape the "cognitive prison" of religion and mythology, he has consigned himself to the prison of materialist and reductive cognition. *Consilience,* exactly like Genesis, explains only what it is capable of explaining. But, unlike Genesis, it concedes nothing to mystery; it simply rules out or blots out whatever it can't explain or doesn't like. One thing it blots out is the damage that this intellectual complacency and condescension has done and is doing still to prescientific cultures and their homelands around the world.

"I mean no disrespect," Mr. Wilson says, "when I say that prescientific people, regardless of their innate genius, could never guess the nature of physical reality beyond the tiny sphere attainable by unaided common sense.... No shaman's spell or fast upon a sacred mountain can summon the electromagnetic spectrum. Prophets of the great religions were kept unaware of its existence, not because of a secretive god but because they lacked the hard-won knowledge of physics" (pp. 46-47). It seems only courteous to inquire at this point if anybody, ever before, has had the originality to propose that the prophets *needed* to know about the electromagnetic spectrum? One may imagine a little play, as follows:

Isaiah *(finger in the air and somewhat oblivious of the historical superiority of the modern audience):* The voice said, Cry. And he said, What shall I cry? All flesh is grass, and all the goodliness thereof is as the flower of the field . . .

Edward O. Wilson *(somewhat impressed, but nonetheless determined to do his bit for "evolutionary progress"):* But . . . But, sir! Are you aware of the existence of the electromagnetic spectrum?

CURTAIN

*

Even as a believer in "the potential of indefinite human progress" (p. 8), Mr. Wilson can be properly humble, when he has the notion. On page 98, for instance, he says that "evolutionary progress is an obvious reality" if we mean by it "the production through time of increasingly complex and controlling organisms and societies, in at least some lines of descent, with regression always a possibility. . . ." One notes with gratitude this consent to the possibility of regression, but in fact Mr. Wilson is not much impressed or detained by any such possibility. Later on, returning to the subject of "preliterate humans," he concedes: "We are all still primitives compared to what we might become." There follows an avowal of the largeness of human ignorance, which, characteristically, he hastens past and quickly forgets: "*Yet* [my emphasis] the great gaps in knowledge are beginning to be filled . . . knowledge continues to expand globally. . . . Any trained person can retrieve and augment any part of it. . . . The explanations can be joined in space from molecule to ecosystem, and in time from microsecond to millenium" (p. 236). And then, speaking as if his program has already been completed, he says, "Now, with science and the arts combined [in consilience], we have it all" (p. 237). Here there is no functioning doubt or question, no live sense of the possibility of regression, no acknowledgment of the possibility that knowledge, if it can be accumulated, can also be lost. There is no hint that knowledge can be misused.

Though his head sometimes tells him that such concessions should be made, his heart never does. In his heart, he is in agreement with the apparent majority of the public who now believe that the new inevitably replaces or invalidates the old, because the new, coming from an ever-growing fund of data, is inevitably better than the old. The rails of the future have been laid by genetic (or technological or economic) determination, and as we move forward we destroy justly and properly the rails of the past. This is strong, easeful, and reassuring doctrine, so long as one does not count its costs or number its losses.

*

If under the demands of a university system obsessively concentrated upon originality and innovation, science serves progress, industry, and the corporate economy, then the literary culture (to use the phrase of C. P. Snow) gives its tacit approval to the program of science-technology-and-industry and, itself, serves nothing — except, perhaps, for certain politically correct ideologies that could be as well served anywhere else. It serves less and less even the cause of literacy, which the university system has made the specialty of the English department, and which the English department has made the specialty of the freshman English program. The university as a whole gives no support to the cause of literacy. If technical or workmanly competence in writing is required only by teachers of freshman English, and virtually all other teachers either require no written work or grade what they do require "on content," then the message is unmistakable: Competence in writing does not matter and is not necessary. And that is what most students believe.

The English department, working under the same dire pressure to "produce" publishable books and articles as every other department, must assign the teaching of English composition to graduate students and a few specialists in the methodology and technology of composition-teaching, while most of the regular faculty concentrate on matters exalted far above grammar and punctuation and sentence structure. One result, as I know from my own experience and observation, is the certification of public school English teachers who do not necessarily know how to construct a coherent English sentence, or punctuate it, or make its nouns and verbs agree, or spell its common English words. Nor is it by any means certain that these certified English teachers will have a sense of literary history and tradition. Another result is the virtual languagelessness of many professional journalists and "communicators." Another is the increasing editorial slovenliness of newspapers and publishing companies.

The cult of progress and the new, along with the pressure to originate, innovate, publish, and attract students, has made the English department as nervously susceptible to fashion as a flock of teenagers. The academic "profession" of literature seems now to be merely tumbling from one critical or ideological fad to another, constantly "revolutionizing" itself in pathetic imitation of the "revolutionary" sciences, issuing all the while a series of passionless, jargonizing, "publishable" but hardly readable articles and books, in which a pretentious obscurity and dullness masquerade as profundity. And this, I think, is not easily definable as the fault of anybody in particular. It is the fault of a bad system—howbeit one that most people in it don't to all appearances object to, and one that nobody in it has effectively objected to. The university's convocation of the disciplines is not a conversation; it is incapable of criticizing itself. One of the most dangerous effects of the specialist system is to externalize its critics, and thus deprive them of standing.

*

Originality and innovation in science may be a danger to the community, because the newness is not inherently good, and because the scientific disciplines use only professional standards in judging their work. There is no real criticism. (Ezra Pound has reminded us that, at root, to criticize is to choose. *ABC of Reading,* p. 30.) Nobody seems able to subtract the negative results of scientific "advances" from the positive. Not many modern scientists would say, with Erwin Chargaff, that "all great scientific discoveries . . . carry . . . an irreversible loss of something that mankind cannot afford to lose" (*Heraclitean Fire,* p. 104). But, then, Chargaff had confronted fully the implication of modern science in the bombing of Hiroshima and Nagasaki and "the German extermination factories." He wrote: "The Nazi experiment in eugenics . . . was the outgrowth of the same kind of mechanistic thinking that, in an outwardly very different form, contributed to what most people would consider the glories of modern science" (*Heraclitean Fire,* pp. 3-5).

In the literary culture, the preponderant aim of originality and innovation strikes directly at the community by granting precedence to intellectual fashion, and so depreciating literacy and literature and the cultural inheritance. The new supposedly dazzles the old out of existence, and people of our era are encouraged to pity their ancestors who had not the good fortune to be as we are. The cult of originality, however, seems to have produced about the expectable amount of bad work, but not much that is truly original.

Instead, it has produced fashions and uniforms of originality. Political correctness becomes the intellectual and literary cutting edge.

One worries that the cultists of the new and original think they are doing what Ezra Pound told them to do. In fact, Pound did say that writers should "make it new," but that was probably as traditional an instruction as he ever gave. It is a statement perhaps too easy to understand as a flippant rejection of the old, but that is not what he meant. Pound used, to begin with, the verb "make," and he, like virtually every poet until recently, knew that our word "poet" came from a Greek word meaning "maker." To make, one must know how to make. And how does one learn? By reading. To Pound, how to write was the same question as how to read. To learn to write one must learn both a considerable portion of what has been written and *how* it was written. And so the first reference of the pronoun in "make it new" is the literary inheritance; one must renew the means of literature, which is to say the literary tradition, by making it newly applicable to contemporary needs and occasions. The new must come from the old, for where else would you get it? Not, anyhow, from contempt for the old, or from ambition. Pound's work, at its sanest, was always a testing of the usefulness of what he had read.

But I think he meant much more than that. There are passages in The *ABC of Reading* that can be understood as glosses on "make it new." "A classic," Pound wrote there, "is classic not because it conforms to certain structural rules, or fits certain definitions.... It is classic because of a certain eternal and irrepressible freshness" (pp. 13-14). And furthermore: "Great literature is simply language charged with meaning to the utmost possible degree" (p. 28).

(Note that he does not use the adjective "new" in that sentence.)
And furthermore: "Literature is news that STAYS news" (p. 29).
The business of literature, then, is to renew not only itself but also
our sense of the perennial newness of the world and of our experience; it is to renew our sense of the newness of what is eternally
new.

Ananda Coomaraswamy, who was a more systematic student of
artistic tradition than Pound, also wrote usefully on the subject of
making it new: "There can be no property in ideas, because these
are gifts of the Spirit, and not to be confused with talents. . . . No
matter how many times [it] may already have been 'applied' by others, whoever conforms himself to an idea and makes it his own, will
be working originally, but not so if he is expressing only his own
ideals or opinions" (*Christian and Oriental Philosophy of Art,
Dover,* 1956, p. 38). And perhaps even more helpfully he wrote that
"when there is realization, when the themes are felt and art *lives,*
it is of no moment whether . . . the themes are new or old" (*The
Transformation of Nature in Art,* Dover, 1956, p. 35). It should be
fairly clear that a culture has taken a downward step when it forsakes the always difficult artistry that renews what is neither new
nor old and replaces it with an artistry that merely exploits what is
fashionably or adventitiously "new," or merely displays the "originality" of the artist.

*

Scientists who believe that "original discovery is everything" justify their work by the "freedom of scientific inquiry," just as would-
be originators and innovators in the literary culture justify their

work by the "freedom of speech" or "academic freedom." Ambition in the arts and the sciences, for several generation now, has conventionally surrounded itself by talk of freedom. But surely it is no dispraise of freedom to point out that it does not exist spontaneously or alone. The hard and binding requirement that freedom must answer, if it is to last, or if in any meaningful sense it is to exist, is that of responsibility. For a long time the originators and innovators of the two cultures have made extravagant use of freedom, and in the process have built up a large debt to responsibility, little of which has been paid, and for most of which there is not even a promissory note.

The debt can be paid only by thought, work, deference, and affection given to the integrity of our ecological and cultural life. The condition which that integrity (or that one-time integrity) imposes on human work and human freedom is that everything we do has an effect or an influence. But it is generally true to say that among the originators of the modern era there has been no flinching before effects, for the purpose of the originators (as understood by themselves) has been the origination of causes only. This is the moral absurdity of specialization driven to the limit. The effects are understood simply as the causes of other original work by other specialists. And thus we have assumed that all problems merely lead to solutions, an article of pathological faith.

All along, the enterprise of science-industry-and-technology has been accompanied by a tradition of objection. Blake's revulsion at the "dark Satanic Mills" and Wordsworth's perception that "we murder to dissect" have been handed down through a succession of lives and works, and among the inheritors have been scientists as well as artists. The worry, I think, has always been that in our ever-accelerating effort to explain, control, use, and sell the world we would destroy the wholeness and the sanctity of all that which it is our highest obligation to "make new."

On the day after Hitler's troops marched into Prague, the Scottish poet Edwin Muir, then living in that city, wrote in his journal a note that recalls a similar lamentation of Montaigne about four hundred years earlier: "So many goodly citties ransacked and razed," Montaigne wrote; "so many nations destroyed and made desolate; so infinite millions of harmelesse people of all sexes, states and ages, massacred, ravaged and put to the sword; and the richest, the fairest and the best part of the world topsiturvied, ruined and defaced for the traffick of Pearles and Pepper: Oh mechanicall victories, oh base conquest" (*Essays,* Everyman, Vol. 3, p. 144). Muir wrote: "Think of all the native tribes and peoples, all the simple indigenous forms of life which Britain trampled upon, corrupted, destroyed . . . in the name of commercial progress. All these things, once valuable, once human, are now dead and rotten. The nineteenth century thought that machinery was a moral force and would make men better. How could the steam-engine make men better? Hitler marching into Prague is connected with all this. If I look back over the last hundred years it seems to me that we have lost more than we have gained, that what we have lost was valuable, and that what we have gained is trifling, for what we have lost was old and what we have gained is merely new" (*The Story and the Fable,* Rowan Tree Press, 1987, p. 257).

Laboring in the shadow of the scientific apocalypse of World War II, C. S. Lewis wrote: "Dreams of the far future destiny of man were dragging up from its shallow and unquiet grave the old dream of Man as God. The very experiences of the dissecting room and the pathological laboratory were breeding a conviction that the stifling of all deep-set repugnances was the first essential for progress" (*That Hideous Strength,* Macmillan Paperback, 1976, p. 203).

Albert Howard, at about the same time rethinking the role of science in agriculture, wrote: "It is a severe question, but one which imposes itself as a matter of public conscience, whether agricultural research in adopting the esoteric attitude, in putting itself above the public and above the farmer whom it professes to serve, in taking refuge in the abstruse heaven of the higher mathematics, has not subconsciously been trying to cover up what must be regarded as a period of ineptitude and of the most colossal failure. Authority has abandoned the task of illuminating the laws of Nature, has forfeited the position of the friendly judge, scarcely now ventures even to adopt the tone of the earnest advocate: it has sunk to the inferior and petty work of photographing the corpse . . ." (*The Soil and Health,* Schocken Books, 1972, p. 81).

And in the autobiographical meditation written when he was old, looking back over the course of science from the time of his own crisis of conscience at the revelations of World War II, Erwin Chargaff wrote: "The wonderful, inconceivably intricate tapestry is being taken apart strand by strand; each thread is being pulled out, torn up, and analyzed; and at the end even the memory of the design is lost and can no longer be recalled" (*Heraclitean Fire,* p. 56).

It is not easily dismissable that virtually from the beginning of the progress of science-technology-and-industry that we call the

Industrial Revolution, while some have been confidently predict-
ing that science, going ahead as it has gone, would solve all problems and answer all questions, others have been in mourning.
Among these mourners have been people of the highest intelligence
and education, who were speaking, not from nostalgia or reaction
or superstitious dread, but from knowledge, hard thought, and the
promptings of culture.

What were they afraid of? What were their "deep-set repugnances"? What did they mourn? Without exception, I think, what
they feared, what they found repugnant, was the violation of life
by an oversimplifying, feelingless utilitarianism; they feared the
destruction of the living integrity of creatures, places, communities, cultures, and human souls; they feared the loss of the old pre-
scriptive definition of humankind, according to which we are neither gods nor beasts, though partaking of the nature of both. What
they mourned was the progressive death of the earth.

Wes Jackson of the Land Institute said once, thinking of the
nuclear power and genetic engineering industries, "We ought to
stay out of the nuclei." I remember that because I felt that he was
voicing, not scientific intelligence, but a wise instinct: an intuition,
common enough among human beings, that some things are and
ought to be forbidden to us, off-limits, unthinkable, foreign, *properly* strange. I remember it furthermore because my own instinctive
wish was to "stay out of the nuclei," and, as I well knew, this wish
amounted exactly to nothing. One can hardly find a better example
of modern science as a public predicament. For modern scientists
work with everybody's proxy, whether or not that proxy has been
given. A good many people, presumably, would have chosen to

"stay out of the nuclei," but that was a choice they did not have. When a few scientists decided to go in, they decided for everybody. This "freedom of scientific inquiry" was immediately transformed into the freedom of corporate and/or governmental exploitation. And so the freedom of the originators and exploiters has become, in effect, the abduction and imprisonment of all the rest of us. Adam was the first, but not the last, to choose for the whole human race.

The specialist system, using only professional standards, thus isolates and overwhelmingly empowers the specialist as the only authorizer of his work—she alone is made the sole moral judge of the need or reason for her work. This solitary assumption of moral authority, of course, must *precede* the acceptance of patronage. Originality as a professional virtue gives far too much importance and power to originators, and at the same time isolates them socially and morally.

*

The specialist within the literary culture is isolated, it seems to me, in precisely the same way, and in fact *wishes* to be so isolated. The effects of the work of the literary specialists are not, of course, so directly practical as those of the scientists, but they are in the long run a part of the same disintegration, and are equally serious.

That the arts have been envious of the prestige, the drama, and the glamour of innovative science is suggested by the long-enduring vogue of "experimental art." "Experiment" is a word that seems displaced and uncomfortable outside of science; in science, I suppose, a failed experiment is still science, but in art a failed experiment, whatever else it may be, is not art. Misnomer or not, "experimentation" in the arts certainly bespeaks a hankering among artists for the heroism of life on the "cutting edge."

The science closest to art (in the opinion, anyhow, of many artists) is psychology and especially psychoanalysis. The study of the "psyche" is not a very exact science, but its subject matter is indigenous to the arts, and it is not hard to understand how attractive among artists have been the psychological theories of consciousness and "the unconscious." The idea of imitating in writing the "stream of consciousness" occurred early to novelists, and the psychoanalysts carried on and encouraged the artists' age-old fascination with dreams.

Maybe because modern artists took so many promptings from psychology, the scientific goal of "original discovery" became in art, and particularly in literature, the goal of original disclosure. It seems generally true that in the twentieth century writers' interest in personal life and in the inward life of persons became more intense, intimate, and in certain ways more articulate than before. The difference, roughly, is that between Tennyson's "Ulysses" and Eliot's "The Love Song of J. Alfred Prufrock." There is a new keenness, or a new kind of keenness, in understanding how people understand themselves.

Along with this interest in the intimate, inward histories of fictional persons has come (in what relation of cause or effect, I don't know) an interest in disclosing the private lives of real persons. Such disclosures are now conventional and commonplace in biography, in "confessional poetry," and in "fictionalized" accounts of actual lives and events. The most inward life is laid open, the most intimate details are shown, exactly as in dissection (which means cutting apart) or autopsy (which means seeing for yourself). One of the paramount originations of the modern literary culture is the discovery that privacy is penetrable and publishable, and that publication is not likely to be legally actionable. In fiction and poetry, in biography, in journalism and the entertainment industry, and finally in politics, the cutting edge for most of the twentieth century has been the dis-covering of the intimate, the secret, the sexual, the private, and the obscene. And this process of exposure has been carried on in the name of freedom by people priding themselves on their courage.

Has it required courage? So long as it involved legal or professional penalties, it most certainly did require courage. But now that the penalties have been removed, no courage is necessary. Public sexual revelations and public obscenity are now merely clichés, part of the uniform behavior of modish nonconformity and fashionable bad manners, but always performed by people who wish to be thought courageous.

Has it increased freedom? Well, of course people have become more free when they have earned or taken or been given the right to do what they previously were forbidden to do. But, as always, the worth of freedom depends upon how it is used. The value of freedom is probably not intrinsic and is certainly not limitless. It is generally understood by people who think about it that freedom can be abused, and that it rests, in the long run, on a common understanding of fairness: One should not increase one's freedom by reducing somebody else's.

I would question also the worth of freedom from what C. S. Lewis called our "deep-set repugnances," among which I would include our native and proper repugnance against nosiness, against having our privacy invaded. This has to do, I think, with our rightful fear of being misunderstood or too simply understood, or of having our profoundest experience misvalued. This, surely, is one of the reasons for Christ's insistence on the privacy of prayer. It is a part of our deepest and most precious integrity that we should speak (if we wish) for ourselves. We do not want self-appointed spokesmen for our souls. Sex and worship especially are inward to us, and they are especially fragile as possessions. Their nature is to be shared, and yet it is dangerous to speak of them carelessly. To speak of them carelessly is to violate yet another nucleus that ought to be sacrosanct.

Our present idea of freedom in science is too often reducible to thoughtlessness of consequence. Freedom in the arts frequently looks like mere carelessness in self-exposure or in exposing others. In both science and art there is a principled resistance to any suggestion that the specialist, within his or her work, might be subject or subordinate to anything.

On October 19, 1998, in New York City, the Authors Guild and the Authors Guild Foundation held a panel discussion, "Whose Life Is It, Anyway?"—a transcript of which was published in the *Authors Guild Bulletin,* Winter 1999, pages 13-26. The panelists, Cynthia Ozick, David Leavitt, Janna Malamud Smith, and Judy Collins, "addressed the moral, ethical and artistic implications of the writer's appropriation of others' lives and experiences." Parts of their conversation are illustrative of the problem of freedom, and I am going to quote from it at some length. Several of my ellipses indicate large omissions.

Cynthia Ozick said: "I could not fathom that fiction might not be an arena of total freedom. . . . I remember sitting on the edge of a bed with my mother-in-law, explaining how I'd been keeping a diary since 1953, and that everyone was in it. She was terrifically disturbed. 'No, no,' she cried, 'erase it, you can't have it, you mustn't do this.' And instantly I realized . . . that no writer could ever take that view. Life becomes real only through having been written. . . . Inevitably, writers are responsible for wounds and hurts—but the writer must say, I don't care, I don't give a damn. . . ."

David Leavitt quoted with approval a writing teacher who once told a class, "For every writer it is a rite of passage to write the story after which a member of your family will no longer speak to you." And later Mr. Leavitt states his credo: "I say anything goes in fiction—anything goes. If you start to take away bit by bit the rights of writers doing what they want, what you end up eroding is your own freedom."

Ms. Ozick agreed that "anything goes." But then she made an exception: "Yet I do have certain lines of limits. . . . I would not admire—I would strenuously object to—a novel which took a Holocaust-denial point of view. . . . But that's an extreme issue. For the writer . . . it's only make-believe, it's the world of enchantment. Make-believe and enchantment can't really harm anyone."

Janna Malamud Smith, politely on the contrary, said this: "When rationalizing their exposure of others, writers tend to claim two values as having overriding worth. One is the aesthetic goal of telling the story well. There's often a feeling that writing beautifully is an ultimate good, that telling a tale very well compensates any harm it might do to its subjects. The second virtue writers tend to honor is outing the truth. We take seriously the job of looking behind hypocrisy and social facade.... We like to believe there is a version of the truth that is superior and that we can state it. These are serious premises.... But I think they thrive best when they are occasionally pruned by opposing values. . . . The reason people feel betrayed when they find themselves in people's books is this: Intimacy . . . works because you are allowed to do things in a friendship, in a love relationship, that you can't do in public. So when the private things intimacy has allowed you to expose are suddenly made public, that is a legitimate reason for a feeling of profound betrayal.... The fact is that betrayals are a real thing."

Later, Ms. Smith speaks of the possibility that people might be "led astray by romantic novels," and she says, "Influence is real, and probably we need to think about that as well."

It certainly is true that writers are burdened with the responsibility to bear witness to such truth as they have seen or think they have seen. The responsibility goes with the trade: There is no value in telling anything if one does not try with all one's might to tell the truth. If human beings could be utterly confident of their ability to tell—or know—the truth, then the problem would be at least smaller, though a writer's insistence upon "total freedom" to tell the truth about other people would still be questionable. Since human beings can be wrong, since even with the best intentions they may know falsely and tell falsehoods, to say that "anything goes" and to leave it at that is far too simple.

My intention here is certainly not to promote any abridgment of the freedoms of speech and inquiry, though I believe that those freedoms are now being pretty severely abused and that the abuse of freedom threatens its survival. But I agree with Janna Malamud Smith that betrayal and influence are real and must be thought about.

I don't believe that the connection between art and life can ever be finally or even very satisfactorily resolved, any more than can be the connection between science and life. We join ourselves to the living world by the artifacts of art and science—by made things. And we are always going to be at least somewhat at fault, because we are ignorant and fallible and small; the living world is larger and more complex than our works. Because we must be always correcting our errors, art and science always need to be free to shift their ground and start again. The unendable, the necessarily ongoing problem of justice to the world and to one another thus enforces practically the requirement of freedom. And this freedom can survive, I believe, only by being well used.

What "well used" may mean was clearly shown by Richard C. Strohman in an article in *The Daily Californian* (April 1, 1999, page 5). Mr. Strohman was writing in defense of "unimpeded science." He was worried about the costs to science of "new initiatives for university-corporate alliances" in the development of biotechnology. The costs, apparently, will be the familiar ones of too much specialization and of a falsifying oversimplification. Mr. Strohman wrote: "The corporate need for technology dedicated to specific products will ... must ... subvert the scientific need for unimpeded research. In academic biology the technological need to define complex behavior in terms of simple causality subverts the need for a wider, more complex research context.

"Here then is the real danger of the university-corporate 'merger' . . . a corporate need that must repress new ways of seeing nature."

And so science too must be concerned with "making it new" and with renewing itself, and now it must do so for a reason both new and urgent: to see that nature escapes the corporations which are newly empowered to oversimplify it, commodify it, and put it up for sale. Mr. Strohman's answer, I think, is the correct one: Enlarge the context of the work.

Freedom in both science and art probably depends upon enlarging the context of our work, increasing (rather than decreasing) the number of considerations we allow to bear upon it. This is because the ultimate context of our work is the world, which is always larger than the context of our thought. And so to complicate the consideration of freedom in literature by the considerations of betrayal and influence is not a diminishment of literature or freedom; it is a *just* enlargement of the context of work. If we could faithfully commit ourselves to the principle that nothing whatever can safely be said to lie outside the context of our work, then artists and scientists would have to be ready at any time to see that they have been wrong and to start again, making yet larger the context of the work. *That* is true freedom. It means simply that beyond all error we can begin again; redemption is possible. From this principle also we can make our way to critical judgments of an amplitude beyond specialization and professionalism: Work that diminishes the possibility of a new start, of "making it new," is bad work.

Janna Malamud Smith said, "You don't trade betrayal for writing . . ." That is not a simple statement, because to be a writer is not a simple predicament. There is a constant relationship, though never altogether settled and never altogether clear, between imagination and reality. If you are a fiction writer, you may, at one extreme, tell a story that is almost the story of something that actually happened; at the opposite extreme, you may tell a story that you have almost entirely imagined. But what you have imagined will always be somewhat informed by what you have actually known, and your actual knowing will always be somewhat informed by imagination. The extremes of reality and imagination, within the limits of human experience, are never pure. And so there is always some risk of betrayal. It is possible to allow imagination to abuse reality; it is possible by imagination to violate a real intimacy — and this leaves aside the possibility of deliberately tattling for meanness or revenge or some version of success. It is always possible too that imagination may be debased by a false or too narrow understanding of what is real.

Both imagination and a competent sense of reality are necessary to our life, and they necessarily discipline one another. Only imagination, for example, can give our home landscape and community a presence in our minds that is a sort of vision at once geographical and historical, practical and protective, affectionate and hopeful. But if that vision is not repeatedly corrected by a fairly accurate sense of reality, if the vision becomes fantastical or merely wishful, then both we and the landscape fall into danger; we may destroy the landscape, or the landscape (especially if damaged by us in our illusion) may destroy us.

To speak of betrayal as a possibility in literature is one way of acknowledging this necessary and inescapable tension between

imagination and reality. Fiction can abuse reality by violating intimacy or confidence or privacy, or by being wrong. Not least among
the offenses of literary artists is their frequent indifference to facts
of history or natural history or ways of work.

To be careless of such betrayals is to reduce one's subject to the
status of "raw material"—exactly as the ubiquitous enterprise of
science-technology-and-industry reduces *its* subjects. The parallels of value and attitude among contemporary arts and sciences
and the industrial economy are obvious, are ratified by convention,
and are almost unnoticed by the would-be pioneers and heroes of
the cutting edges. But if one lives, as I do, in a rural place, which is
to say in the midst of other people's "raw material," then one does
notice. And if one notices, then one knows that artistic and scientific betrayals are real and are serious. They are an affront to one's
subject, and they endanger it.

Too much disclosure of the intimate, the secret, the sexual, the
private, and the obscene is accomplished by mentioning or repre-
senting or picturing but not imagining. To represent the intimacy
of desire or of grief without the art that compels one to imagine
these things as the events of lives and of shared lives is actually to
misrepresent them. This is the "objectivity" of the schools and the
professions, which allows a university or a corporation to look at
the community—its *own* community—as one looks at a distant
landscape through fog. This sort of objectivity functions in art
much the same as in science; it obstructs compassion; it obscures
the particularity of creatures and places. In both, it is a failure of
imagination.

Journalism and the electronic media, for example, routinely exhibit representations or disclosures of intimate emotion as objects of curiosity, as intrinsically interesting, or as proofs of artistic or journalistic courage. The perennial act of cutting-edge enterprise in reporting is to shove a camera or a microphone into the face of a grieving woman. But what is the qualitative difference between the man who cold-heartedly shoots another and the photographer who cold-heartedly photographs the corpse or the grieving widow? Are they not simply two parts of the same epidemic failure of imagination, which is to say a failure of compassion and of community life?

Such exposures do not make us free, and they do not increase our knowledge. They only compound human cruelty by a self-induced numbness to the suffering of others and to our common suffering.

To be indifferent to hurts given by one's writing to its human subjects, which exactly parallels the scientific-industrial indifference to the suffering of animal or human subjects of exploitation or experimentation—to say "I don't care, I don't give a damn"—is a betrayal not only of the subject of writing, which is invariably our common life, our neighborhood, but also of imagination itself. It is a refusal to be compassionate, a denial of the vital link between imagination and compassion. How can such a betrayal not impair one's ability to know the truth and to make art?

The world and its neighborhoods, natural and human, are not passively the subjects of art, any more than they are passively the subjects of science-industry-and-technology. They are affected by all that we do. And they respond. The world does not exist merely to be written about, any more than it exists merely to be studied. It is real, before and after human work. What we write is finally to be measured by the health of what we write about. What we think we know affects the health of the thing we think we know.

The problem of influence also is real, and it is inescapable. Ms. Ozick acknowledges as much when she wishes to exempt the Holocaust from her credo of not giving a damn, and so she undermines all her affirmation of artistic superiority and autonomy. To say that writing about the Holocaust may be influential is to say that writing may be influential, period. Who can deny that writing about Jews with contempt may cause them to be treated with contempt, or with violence? But the history of oppression forbids us to limit that liability to the Jews. We treat people, places, and things in accordance with the way we perceive them, and literature influences our perceptions. To leave aside more fashionable examples, who can deny that the history of coal mining in the southern Appalachians has been under the influence of writers who have written of the mountaineers as "briars" or "hillbillies"? And who wishes to say that our long exploitation and finally our virtual destruction of our farm population has not been influenced by generations of writers who have represented farmers as "yokels" who live in the "sticks" and do "mind-numbing work"? We can't deny that writing has an influence unless we can also deny that stereotyping and character assassination have an influence.

*

The question for art, then, is exactly the same as the question for science: Can it properly subordinate itself to concerns that are larger than its own? Can it judge itself by standards that are higher and more comprehensive than professional standards? The issue is the old one of propriety. Is every artist and every scientist to be "free" to work as if his or her discipline were the only one, or the dominant one? Or is it possible still to see one's work as occurring within a larger and ultimately a mysterious pattern of causes and influences? If we can see that we are mutually dependent upon one another and upon that mosaic of natural and human neighborhoods we call "the world," then it should not be too hard to see that there ought to be responsible connections between science and the knowledge of how to live, and between art and the art of living, and that there is always, inescapably, acknowledged or not, a complex connection between art and science.

7. Progress Without Subtraction

The task of thinking about Mr. Wilson's book is made difficult at every point by his adherence to the rather simple-minded popular doctrine of mechanical or automatic progress. His book perhaps was written as a defense of that doctrine. He believes, with the Enlightenment thinkers, in "the potential of indefinite human progress" (p. 8). He affirms the necessity to speak of "evolutionary progress" (p. 98). In spite of his perfunctory acknowledgment of the possibility of regression (p. 98) he speaks twice (pp. 270 and 289) of the "Ratchet of Progress." He says that "humanity accepted the Ratchet of Progress" (p. 270) as if to suggest that we had a choice, but he doesn't say what we might have accepted instead. The practical effect of his belief in the inevitability of progress is to make him a poor critic of his own thought. In fact, for all his enthusiasm, he is a rather passive consumer of scientific platitudes. His idea of progress, for example, is both starkly deterministic (it is "evolutionary" and a "ratchet") and hazily romantic: Modern science, he says, is "driven by the faith that if we dream, press to discover, explain, and dream again, thereby plunging repeatedly into new terrain, the world will somehow come clearer and we will grasp the true strangeness of the universe. And the strangeness will all prove to be connected and make sense" (p. 12). Later, in his very sobering appraisal of our destruction of "the environment," he says, "We must plunge ahead and make the best of it, worried but confident of success . . ." (p. 289).

This is utterly baffling. If our future is already determined by "evolutionary progress" and the "ratchet" is in place, there is no use in "plunging" anywhere—unless it is to exercise our "biologically adaptive" "illusion of free will." But if free will is an illusion, to what purpose do we make the world clearer? What Mr. Wilson evidently means by "plunging" is merely going ahead as we are going with our "really important research" and "following patronage." It is hard to see how any of this could be encouraging or useful to a conservationist.

If regression really is a possibility, then should we not watch for the signs of it? And should we not attempt to subtract regression from progression to get at least an approximate notion of net gain or net loss? Mr. Wilson concedes that people forget and die, but he says that "knowledge continues to expand globally while passing from one generation to the next" (p. 236). But in fact as knowledge expands globally it is being lost locally. This is the paramount truth of the modern history of rural places everywhere in the world. And it is the gravest problem of land use: Modern humans typically are using places whose nature they have never known and whose history they have forgotten; thus ignorant, they almost necessarily abuse what they use. If science has sponsored both an immensity of knowledge and an immensity of violence, what is the gain? If we "grasp the true strangeness of the universe" but forget how to farm, what is the gain?

Such questions, seriously asked and intelligently answered, lead directly to choices that people have the ability to make, but no such possibility is suggested in *Consilience*.

In Edward O. Wilson's view, the world is not a place where we all make in our daily lives intelligent or unintelligent choices affecting the future of the world. It is, rather, a place where the most genetically favored and the most richly subsidized scientists determine the future by "plunging ahead," each isolated in his or her vision of "new terrain," and each cut off from any restraining affection for old terrain.

Why should we trust them?

IV. Reduction and Religion

IT IS CLEARLY bad for the sciences and the arts to be divided into "two cultures." It is bad for scientists to be working without a sense of obligation to cultural tradition. It is bad for artists and scholars in the humanities to be working without a sense of obligation to the world beyond the artifacts of culture. It is bad for both of these cultures to be operating strictly according to "professional standards," without local affection or community responsibility, much less any vision of an eternal order to which we all are subordinate and under obligation. It is even worse that we are actually confronting, not just "two cultures," but a whole ragbag of disciplines and professions, each with its own jargon more or less unintelligible to the others, and all saying of the rest of the world, "That is not my field."

The badness of all this is manifested first in the loss even of the pretense of intellectual or academic community. This is a loss increasingly ominous because intellectual engagement among the disciplines, across the lines of the specializations—that is to say *real* conversation—would enlarge the context of work; it would press thought toward a just complexity; it would work as a system of checks and balances, introducing criticism that would reach beyond the professional standards. Without such a vigorous conversation originating in the universities and emanating from them, we get what we've got: sciences that spread their effects upon the world as if the world were no more than an experimental laboratory; arts and "humanities" as unmindful of their influence as if the world did not exist; institutions of learning whose chief purpose is to acquire funds and be administered by administrators; governments whose chief purpose is to provide offices to members of political parties.

The ultimate manifestation of this incoherence is loss of trust—loss, moreover, of the entire cultural pattern by which we understand what it means to give and receive trust. The general assumption now is that everybody is working in his or her own interest and will continue to do so until checked by somebody whose self-interest is more powerful. That nobody now trusts the politicians or their governments is probably the noisiest of present facts. More quietly, people are withdrawing their trust from the professions, the corporations, the education system, the religious institutions, the medical industry. Perhaps no expert has yet assigned a quantitative value to trust; it is nonetheless certain that when we have finished subtracting trust from all we think we have gained, not much will be left.

And so it certainly is desirable—it probably is necessary—that the arts and the sciences should cease to be "two cultures" and become fully communicating, if not always fully cooperating, parts of one culture. (I believe, as I will show, that this culture when it comes will be in fact a mosaic of cultures, based upon every community's recognition that all its members have a common ground, and that this ground is the ground under their feet.) I have, therefore, not the slightest inclination to disagree with Mr. Wilson's wish for a "linkage of the arts and humanities." With his goal of "consilience," though I sympathize, I do not agree.

I do not agree because I do not think it is possible. I do not think it is possible because, as he defines it, it would impose the scientific methodology of reductionism upon cultural properties, such as religion and the arts, that are inherently alien to it, and that are often expressly resistant to reduction of any kind. Consilience, Mr. Wilson says, is "literally a 'jumping together' of knowledge by the linking of facts and fact-based theory across disciplines to create a common groundwork of explanation" (p. 8). And: "The only way either to establish or to refute consilience is by methods developed in the natural sciences—not . . . an effort led by scientists, or frozen in mathematical abstraction, but rather one allegiant to the habits of thought that have worked so well in exploring the material universe" (p. 9). The project of consilience, then, is not for scientists only, but it is only for science.

Whether or not science, religion, and the arts can be linked on "a common groundwork of explanation" depends upon a further question: Can religion and the arts be explained in the same way that science can be, or can they, in any comprehensive way, be explained at all? And this, it seems to me, depends upon another question that is even more important: Is knowledge by definition explainable, or is there such a thing as unexplainable knowledge?

I have in mind three statements that seem to me to test this issue of knowledge and explainability:

At the end of *King Lear,* the broken-hearted old king comes in with his faithful daughter Cordelia dead in his arms. He says: "Thou'lt come no more, / Never never never never never." (v, iii, 308-309)

In II Samuel 18:33, David the king has just been told that his son, who has been his enemy, is dead. The King says: "O my son Absalom, my son, my son Absalom! would God I had died for thee, O Absalom, my son, my son!"

After the battle of Gettysburg, General Lee was overheard saying to himself, "Too bad! Too bad! Oh, too bad!" (*Lee,* an abridgement by Richard Harwell of the four-volume *R. E. Lee* by Douglas Southall Freeman, Scribner, 1961, p. 341)

These outcries "out of the depths" certainly express knowledge, and precisely too. They communicate knowledge. But the knowledge they convey cannot be proved, demonstrated, or explained; it cannot be taught or learned. These utterances are not "self-explanatory." They are as far as possible unlike what we now call "information." One either does or does not know what they mean. The idea of explaining them to someone who does not know is merely laughable.

Statements of religious faith seem to me to be of the same general kind. Job says: "I know that my redeemer liveth, and that he shall stand at the latter day upon the earth: And though . . . worms destroy this body, yet in my flesh shall I see God . . ." (19:25-26).

This statement rests upon no evidence, no proof. It is not in any respectable sense a theory. Job calls it knowledge: He "knows" that what he says is true. A great many people who have read these verses have agreed; they too have known that this is so.

"The empiricist" in Mr. Wilson's chapter on "Ethics and Religion" would find Job's knowledge readily explainable as a "beneficent" falsehood, supported by no "objective evidence" or "statistical proofs" (pp. 243-245). Mr. Wilson himself understands it as a genetically implanted "urge": "Perhaps . . . it can all eventually be explained as brain circuitry and deep, genetic history" (p. 261). People follow religion, he says, because it is "easier" than empiricism (p. 262), the lab evidently being harder to bear than the cross. Mr. Wilson forgets, in calling attention to religion's want of statistical proofs, that empiricism can supply no statistical disproofs. His explanation of religion rather tends to prove that it is not explainable. God and the devices of human understanding are not the same subject.

Suppose, granting the hopelessness of empirical proof, that you took Job's statement of faith as seriously as Mr. Wilson wishes you to take empiricism; how, then, could you explain it to Mr. Wilson? It seems to me that you would have to concede—and here empirical evidence is available—that it could not be done.

His statement of his own "position" brings no clarification; though it is a statement of a faith somewhat less than scientific, for it has no proofs, it carefully does not touch the issue of religious faith: "I am an empiricist. On religion I lean toward deism but consider its proof largely *a problem* in astrophysics. The existence of a cosmological God who created the universe (as envisioned by

deism) is *possible,* and *may eventually* be settled, *perhaps* by forms
of material evidence *not yet* imagined. Or the matter may be forever
beyond human reach. In contrast . . . the existence of a biological
God, one who directs organic evolution and intervenes in human
affairs (as envisioned by theism) is *increasingly* contravened by
biology and the brain sciences" (pp. 240-241). My emphases call
attention to the extreme tentativeness of the thought. Mr. Wilson
concedes on the same page, "I may be wrong," but that very con-
cession exposes the hopelessness of the argument that he is proposing to settle by consilience. How could he be "proven" wrong?
The faith of an empirical deist will probably have to wait a good
while for proof or disproof by astrophysics. About as long, I imagine, as it will take the "increasing" evidence of biology and the
brain sciences to culminate in empirical disproof of theism.

What is the difference between an "empirical" faith so hedged
about and religious faith? One difference, to use Edwin Muir's
terms, is that whereas religious faith is old, the empirical faith is
merely new. A second difference is that religious faith has lived to
grow old because to hundreds of generations it has appeared to
rest upon a knowledge that is not empirical, whereas the empirical
faith, as its language shows, rests only upon speculation.

There is no reason, as I hope and believe, that science and religion might not live together in amity and peace, so long as they
both acknowledge their real differences and each remains within
its own competence. Religion, that is, should not attempt to dis-
pute what science has actually proved; and science should not
claim to know what it does not know, it should not confuse theory
and knowledge, and it should disavow any claim on what is empirically unknowable.

The two cannot be reconciled by Mr. Wilson's consilience because consilience requires the acceptance of empiricism as a ruling dogma or orthodoxy, denying standing or consideration to any thought not subject to empirical proof. His proposed consilience, by attempting to impose on art and religion the methods and values of reductive science, would prolong the disunity and disintegration it is meant to heal. Like a naive politician, Mr. Wilson thinks he has found a way to reconcile two sides without realizing that his way is one of the sides. There is simply no reason for any person of faith to discuss consilience with Mr. Wilson. One cannot, in honesty, propose to reconcile Heaven and Earth by denying the existence of Heaven.

The danger of this sort of reconciliation, as twentieth-century politics has shown, is that whatever proposes to invalidate or abolish religion (and this is what consilience pretty openly proposes) is in fact attempting to put itself in religion's place. Science-as-religion is clearly a potent threat to freedom. Beyond that, it endangers real science. Science can function as religion only by making two unscientific claims: that it will *eventually* know everything, and that it will *eventually* solve all human problems. And here it is enough to note that at times Mr. Wilson allows the term "science" to become altogether too elastic.

Religion, as empiricists must finally grant, deals with a reality beyond the reach of empiricism. This larger reality does not manifest itself in the manner of laboratory results or in the manner of a newspaper front page. Christ does not come down from the cross and confound his tormentors, as good a movie as that would make. God does not speak loudly from Heaven in the most popular modern languages for all to hear. (If He did, we would have no need for science, or religion either.) It is nevertheless true that people believe in the existence of this larger reality, and accept religious truth as knowledge, because of their *experience*. John Milton, to whom Mr. Wilson so easily condescends, is only one of many poets in our tradition who wrote of an unevident reality, and who invoked the muse for aid in so great a task. The walls of the rational, empirical world are famously porous. What come through are dreams, imaginings, inspirations, visions, revelations. There is no use in stooping over these with a magnifying lens. Beyond any earthly reason we experience beauty in excess of use, justice in excess of anger, mercy in excess of justice, love in excess of deserving or fulfillment. We have known evil beyond imagining and seemingly beyond intention. We have known compassion and forgiveness beyond measure. And all of this is in excess of what Mr. Wilson means by "religion" and of what he means by "ethics."

Religion, it seems to me, has dealt with this reality clumsily enough, and that is why the history of a religion and its organizations is so frequently a blight on its teachings. But religion at least attempts to deal with religious experience on its own terms; it does not try to explain it by terms that are fundamentally alien to it. For thousands of years, for example, people (who were not dummies) have supposed that dreams come from outside the waking world, speaking to us at least some of the time, and however unclearly, of a reality beyond that world. Hamlet speaks for a lot of people, and very much to my point, when he says, "I could be bounded in a nutshell and count myself a king of infinite space were it not that I have bad dreams" (II, ii, 260-262). The same, of course, is true of good dreams. Mr. Wilson says, typically, that "dreaming is a kind of insanity, a rush of visions, largely unconnected to reality . . . arbitrary in content . . . very likely a side effect of the reorganization and editing of information in the memory banks of the brain" (p. 75). Something of the sort, of course, may be said of inspiration, imagination, beauty, justice, mercy, and love—which consilience would require us to understand as mere strategies of survival encoded in our genes. But this kind of reduction is sufficiently answered by the fact that these things, thus explained, are no longer even conceptually what they were. Reduction does not necessarily limit itself to compacting and organizing knowledge; it also has the power to change what is known.

But biblical religion (which is the only religion that Mr. Wilson talks about) is also explicitly against reductionism. Mr. Wilson's spokesman "the empiricist" hauls out, as if he had thought of it himself, the most popular "environmental" cliché about Christianity: "With a second life waiting, suffering can be endured—especially in other people. The natural environment can be used up" (p. 245). This little platitude has passed from mouth to mouth for years, chewable but not swallowable. It is untrue. Nobody who has actually read the Gospels could believe it. It ignores the very point of the Incarnation. It ignores Christ's unfailing compassion for sufferers, whom He healed, one by one, as they came or were carried to Him. And there is nowhere in the Bible a single line that gives or implies a permission to "use up" the "natural environment."

On the contrary, the Bible says that between all creatures and God there is an absolute intimacy. All flesh lives by the spirit and breath of God (Job 34:14-15). We "live, and move, and have our being" in God (Acts 17:28). In the Gospels it is a principle of faith that God's love for the world includes *every* creature individually, not just races or species. God knows of the fall of every sparrow; He has numbered "the very hairs of your head" (Matthew 10:29-30). Edgar was being perfectly scriptural when he said to his father, "Thy life's a miracle," and so was William Blake when he said that "everything that lives is holy" (*Complete Writings,* p. 160). Julian of Norwich also was following scripture when she said that God "wants us to know that not only does he care for great and noble things, but equally for little and small, lowly and simple things as well" (*Revelations of Divine Love,* Chapter 32). Stephanie Mills is witness to the survival of this tradition when she writes: *"A Sand County Almanac* is suffused with affection for distinct beings . . ." (*In Service of the Wild,* p. 94).

No attentive reader of the Bible can fail to see the writers' alertness to the individuality of things. The characters of humans are sharply observed and are appreciated for their unique qualities. And surely nobody, having read of him once, can forget the war-horse in Job 39:25, who "saith among the trumpets, Ha, ha." I don't know where you could find characterizations more deft and astute than those in the story of the resurrection in John 20:1-17. And again and again the biblical writers write of their pleasure and wonder in the "manifold" works of God, all keenly observed.

People who blame the Bible for the modern destruction of nature have failed to see its delight in the variety and individuality of creatures and its insistence upon their holiness. But that delight—in, say, the final chapters of Job or the 104th psalm—is far more useful to the cause of conservation than the undifferentiating abstractions of science. Empiricists fail to see how the language of religion (and I mean such language as I have quoted, not pulpit clichés) can speak of a non-empirical reality and convey knowledge, and how it can instruct those who use it in good faith. Reverence gives standing to creatures, and to our perception of them, just as the law gives standing to a citizen. Certain things appear only in certain lights. "The gods' presence in the world," Herakleitos said, "goes unnoticed by men who do not believe in the gods" (Guy Davenport, *Herakleitos and Diogenes,* Grey Fox, 1979, p. 21). To define knowledge as merely empirical is to limit one's ability to know; it enfeebles one's ability to feel and think.

We have come face to face with a paradox that we had better notice. Mr. Wilson's materialism is theoretical and reductionistic, tending, in his idea of consilience, toward "unity" (p. 8). People of faith, on the other hand, have always believed in the unity of truth in God, whose works are endlessly and countlessly various. There is a world of difference between this humanly unknowable unity of truth and Mr. Wilson's theoretical unity of knowledge, which supposes that mere humans can know, in some definitive or final way, the truth. And the results are wonderfully different: Acceptance of the mystery of unitary truth in God leads to glorification of the multiplicity of His works, whereas Mr. Wilson's goal of a cognitive unity produced by science leads to abstraction and reduction, the opposite of which is not synthesis. The principle that is opposite to reduction—and, when necessary, its sufficient answer—is God's love for all things, for each thing for its own sake and not for its category.

v. Reduction and Art

By "THE ARTS" Mr. Wilson means "the creative arts, the personal productions of literature, visual arts, drama, music, and dance marked by those qualities which . . . we call the true and the beautiful" (p. 210). He says further that "The defining quality of the arts is the expression of the human condition by mood and feeling, calling into play all the senses, evoking both order and disorder" (p. 213). And he makes a strict distinction between science and the arts: "While biology has an important part to play in scholarly interpretation, the creative arts themselves can never be locked in by this or any other discipline of science. The reason is that the exclusive role of the arts is the transmission of the intricate details of human experience by artifice to intensify aesthetic and emotional response. Works of art communicate feeling directly from mind to mind, with no intent to explain why the impact occurs. In this defining quality, the arts are the antithesis of science.

When addressing human nature, science is coarse-grained and encompassing, as opposed to the arts, which are fine-grained and interstitial. That is, science aims to create principles and use them in human biology to define the diagnostic qualities of the species; the arts use fine details to flesh out and make strikingly clear by implication those same qualities" (pp. 218-219).

These proposed differences notwithstanding, Mr. Wilson argues that science and the arts can be brought into alignment or unity by "consilient explanation." The means of consilience is to be interpretation, which is "the logical channel of consilient explanation between science and the arts" (p. 211). Two questions about the arts are "the central concern of interpretation": "where they come from in both history and personal experience, and how their essential qualities of truth and beauty are to be described through ordinary language" (p. 210). Interpretation of the arts needs to be reinvigorated "with the knowledge of science and its proprietary sense of the future" (p. 211). Mr. Wilson expects that, thus reinvigorated, interpretation will finally show (whether theoretically or by proof is not clear to me) that the arts originate in "an inborn human nature"—that is, in "the material processes of the human mind" (p. 216). Again, the mind is equated with the brain; the consilient explanation of the arts depends upon the explanation of the brain:

"If the brain is ever to be charted and an enduring theory of the arts created as a part of the enterprise, it will be by stepwise and consilient contributions from the brain sciences, psychology, and evolutionary biology. And if during this process the creative mind is to be understood, it will need collaboration between scientists and humanities scholars.

"The collaboration, now in its early stages, is likely to conclude that innovation is a concrete biological process founded upon an intricacy of nerve circuitry and neuro-transmitter release" (p. 216).

Great artists are genetically gifted, not by "singular neurobiological traits," but rather "by a quantitative edge in powers shared in smaller degree with those less gifted," and this quantitative edge produces works that are "qualitatively new" (p. 213). Art is to be accounted for both by genetic evolution and by cultural evolution, but cultural evolution is under the sway of "epigenetic rules of human nature" that draw creative minds toward "certain thoughts and behavior," which, in turn, "bias cultural evolution toward the invention of archetypes, the widely recurring abstractions and core narratives that are dominant themes in the arts" (pp. 217-218 and 223). The most enduring works of art are those that are truest to their origins in human nature: "It follows that even the greatest works of art might be understood fundamentally with knowledge of the biologically evolved epigenetic rules that guided them" (p. 213).

Having tried conscientiously to summarize Mr. Wilson's "working hypothesis" of "the biological origin of the arts" (p. 229), I find a residue of statements that I don't understand well enough to include in my summary. For example, on page 218, he says, *"The arts are innately focused toward certain forms and themes but are otherwise freely constructed"* [his italics]. If the forms and themes, especially the forms, are determined by innate predisposition, then it is not clear how much latitude there can be for freedom of construction. What is called for, apparently, is a sample analysis of a work of art, showing what is "innate" and what is "freely constructed," and how the innate and the free can be conjoined in a work that is "qualitatively new" when innovation has already been described as "a concrete biological process."

Nor am I able to understand the statement that the quality of the arts "is measured by . . . the precision of their adherence to human nature" (p. 226). If the forms and themes of the arts are determined by "an inborn human nature" ("the material processes of the human mind"), then how could they not adhere to it? In a naturally determined system, how can anything happen, or how is anything conceivable, that is unnatural? We need now an example of a work of art that does not adhere to human nature—which, if produced, would testify to the authenticity of that freedom of will which Mr. Wilson has said is illusory. But in a system of biological determinism, how does the issue of quality arise in the first place? If everything is originated biologically and free will is an illusion, then what we get is what we've got, qualitative standards are irrelevant, and critical judgment also is an illusion.

*

But even the parts of Mr. Wilson's "working hypothesis" that I am able to comprehend are frequently in error.

He is much mistaken, to begin with, in his wish to limit the arts to "expression of the human condition by mood and feeling" and to "aesthetic and emotional response." The arts, of course, "express" by their native means: words, colors, shapes, sounds, etc. They also include knowledge. They can instruct. Literature, at least, can convey facts, adduce evidence, and make arguments. *Paradise Lost,* which is the only work of literature that Mr. Wilson discusses at length, is for his thesis particularly unfortunate. Milton's purpose in that poem was avowedly *not* to express the human condition by mood and feeling. His purpose was, as he said, to "assert Eternal Providence, / And justifie the wayes of God to men" (I, 25-26). His poem is, among much else, a great argument. If you read *Paradise Lost,* you will certainly be obliged to feel and to experience moods and to respond aesthetically and emotionally, but you will also have to employ all of your mind to think and comprehend and to make critical judgments. Milton would have been indignant at the suggestion that his art was in any exclusive way "the antithesis of science."

Mr. Wilson would like to exclude science from art, which is easy to do, maybe, in theory, but harder in practice, when one considers how much the arts have been influenced by science and how often science has provided the subject matter of art. It would be a daunting critical exercise to subtract astronomy from *The Divine Comedy,* or biology from *Walden.*

But he would also like to exclude art from science. Though he speaks of the need for "collaboration between scientists and humanities scholars," it is hard to see what use he would have for the humanities scholars, except maybe to provide a little bibliography. His "working hypothesis" of "the biological origin of the arts" is strictly a scientific hypothesis, and it proposes only scientific tasks. Mr. Wilson's councils obviously could not include any humanities scholars who might, for example, take seriously Milton's faith, or his poetic purpose, or his invocation to the Heavenly Muse. The humanities scholars of choice would be those who would affirm Mr. Wilson's materialism, in which case Milton (and a host of other artists) would not be represented or would be misrepresented.

Since Mr. Wilson sees the arts as products of "gene-culture coevolution," he naturally sees them as serving the cause of "survival and reproduction" (pp. 224-226). I am happy to concede him this point. Though I am not much impressed by evolution as the ultimate explanation of life, I am altogether convinced that the arts have helped us to survive and reproduce; to believe otherwise, I would have to deny the existence and the efficacy of love songs. But species survival alone does not adequately account for the existence of the arts, and (if quality is an issue) it does not provide an adequate standard of art criticism. "Survival value," it seems to me, must deal in minimums, since any species dependent upon maximums would be too vulnerable to survive. The human race has survived because of its ability to survive famine, not because of its ability to survive feasts. Survival is possible at minimal levels— in poverty, exile, concentration camps—and this ability merely to persist and endure undoubtedly owes much to instinct, to "inborn human nature," unlearned. But surviving is not the same thing, it is not as high an accomplishment, as the desire to go on living one's own life after surviving, say, defeat or famine or poverty or illness or grief. To live at a high level, desiring and aspiring throughout a human lifetime with its inevitable griefs and troubles, requires culture that, beyond any genetic determination or epigenetic rules, must be deliberately taught and learned. Obviously, the desire to live at a high level can have "survival value" also. Nevertheless, the desire to survive and the desire to live are two different desires, and the second is more conscious, more deliberate, more a matter of education and cultural choice than the first.

Mr. Wilson speaks of human nature as if it were *only* inborn, a product only of evolution. And so he has little choice but to speak of art in the same way. His fundamental error, in proposing his consilience of science and art, is his assumption that works of art are properties of nature in the same way that organisms are. (He thus extends his reductive formula to read: work of art = organism = machine.) He understands works of art as the products of "talent," not as artifacts, not as things made by arts which exist by being taught and learned. Once, on page 213, he says that the masters of the arts have "exceptional knowledge" and "technical skill," but nowhere does he speak of the cultural continuum by which such knowledge and skill are kept alive and handed down. He is interested almost exclusively in the artists' "talent" and their "intuitive grasp of inborn human nature" (p. 213). He does not understand the arts as ways of making or works of art as made things. He asks two questions about the arts: where they come from and how their qualities can be described; he does not ask how they are made. And so he can think of the arts and human nature merely as "natural." He thinks of human nature as "inborn," not as both inborn and to be learned from (among other things) works of art. If human nature (and therefore all its manifestations, such as the arts) is merely natural or inborn, then it is merely a subject of study; no standards of judgment are necessary. If human nature is also the product of learning and is to some extent made by art, then critical judgment is both possible and necessary, and we must deal with issues of will and choice. We are ready to ask, for example, what may be the effect of our cultural and artistic choices upon the natural world. And at this point we can see the error of segregating the "fine" or "creative" arts from the arts that are practical or economic.

Why should our universities sponsor an active criticism of the fine arts (by specialized or professional standards, ignoring their effect on the world) but no criticism of farming or forestry or mining or manufacturing? This question, of course, can be answered by a crude evolutionism—those who survive do not bite the corporations that feed them—but it ought to give some anxiety to a conservationist.

Finally, if innovation (the "qualitatively new") is a primary requirement for art, then why are we still interested in works that are no longer new?

*

Can science and the arts be "linked" by "a common groundwork of explanation"? The answer depends upon the extent to which the arts are reducible to explanation. Mr. Wilson's project of consilience depends upon his assumption that works of art can be rendered into "interpretations" that can then be aligned with the laws of biology and ultimately with the laws of physics. He assumes, in other words, that a sufficient response to a work of art is to "interpret" it, and moreover that the resulting interpretation is as good as or is equal to the work of art. He says that "criticism can be as inspired and idiosyncratic as the work it addresses" (p. 210). (It is consistent with his view of things that he should both deny the possibility of inspiration and use "inspired" as a term of praise, but how he reconciles the supposed intellectual virtue of idiosyncrasy with his zeal for reduction to laws and principles is not clear.) To propose that the value of a work of art lies in its interpretation is to propose further that it is of interest only as an instance or specimen and that it can be not only explained but explained away.

And of course this would be all right if works of art were so constructed as to have extractable meanings or principles or laws. The problem is that they are not so constructed, and in this way they are in fact much like organisms. A chickadee is not constructed to exemplify the principles of its anatomy or the laws of aerodynamics or the life history of its species, and it has not been explained when these things have been extracted (or subtracted) from it.

For a while, in thinking of this question, I proposed to myself that the only things really explainable are explanations. That is not quite true, but it is near enough to the truth that I am unwilling to forget it.

What can be explained? Experiments, ideas, patterns, cause-effect relationships and connections *within defined limits,* anything that can be calculated, graphed, or diagrammed. And yet explanation changes whatever is explained into something explainable. Explanation is reductive, not comprehensive; most of the time, when you have explained something, you discover leftovers. An explanation is a bucket, not a well.

What can't be explained? I don't think creatures can be explained. I don't think lives can be explained. What we know about creatures and lives must be pictured or told or sung or danced. And I don't think pictures or stories or songs or dances can be explained. The arts are indispensable precisely because they are so nearly antithetical to explanation.

The arts are constitutionally resistant to the reduction that Mr. Wilson wishes to subject them to. This resistance manifests itself in two ways: Art insists upon the irreducibility of its subjects; and works of art, as objects, are by nature not reducible.

The power of art tends to be an individuating power, and that tendency is itself an affirmation of the value of individuals and of individuality. It is true that in our literature we have some allegories such as the play *Everyman* and *Pilgrim's Progress,* in which the characters represent abstractions, but this genre, though it contains important works, is a minor one. The dominant flow of our artistic tradition rises from the Bible and from Homer's epics, great works of individualization, which pause to delineate the characters not just of heroes and seers but also of children, housewives, bureaucrats, prostitutes, and tax collectors, of swineherds and old nurses and animals. This tradition, both sacred and democratic, has given us Odysseus and Penelope, Eumaios and Eurykleia, King David and Mary Magdalene, the Wife of Bath, Dante and Virgil, King Lear and Rosalind, Corin the shepherd and Falstaff, Tom Jones, Emma Woodhouse and Mr. Knightley, Captain Ahab, Huckleberry Finn, Tess of the D'Urbervilles, Leopold and Molly Bloom, Joe Christmas and Lena Grove. However much these characters may "stand for" us humans in our quests, flights, trials, and follies, they are each also intransigently themselves, and are valued as such. They all come out of the common fund of human experience, and so we recognize them, but not one of them is the same as anybody else. This tradition gives us the true-to-life portraits of shepherds in Flemish nativity scenes. It is realized pointedly in many a painting of the Virgin, in which she is represented both as the mother of Christ and as whatever ordinary girl posed for the artist.

The truest tendency of art is toward the exaltation, not the reduction, of its subjects. The highest art, as William Blake said, is able

> To see a World in a Grain of Sand
> And a Heaven in a Wild Flower
> (*Complete Writings*, p. 431)

To paint a convincing portrait of the Virgin is to realize that for Christ to be born into this world He had to have a human mother. To write believably of a pilgrimage from Hell to Heaven, or of the transfiguring destitution of Gloucester and Lear, is to require time to remember eternity. Mr. Wilson's science, on the contrary, cannot see a world in a grain of sand. It can classify, name, and (within limits) explain a grain of sand, and divide it into ever smaller parts. There is no reason to say that this work is not admirable, valuable, or useful. But there is reason to say that it is not equivalent to, and it does not replace, the imagination of William Blake. Blake's lines remind us again of the miraculousness of life. This news has been delivered to us time after time in our long tradition. It cannot be proved. It only can be told or shown.

*

All art that rises above competence insists upon the irreducibility of its subjects, its materials, and its finished works. It makes things that are inherently valuable in themselves and are not interchangeable with other things. To a merely competent carpenter, one sound board may be pretty much the same as another. But to a fine carpenter or cabinetmaker, every board is unique. The better artist a woodworker becomes, the more aware he or she becomes of the individuality of boards and of the differences between them. The increase of art accounts for the increase of perception.

In the same way, to be competent a farmer must know the nature of species and breeds of animals. But the better the farmer, the more aware he or she is of the animals' individuality. "Every one is different," you hear the good stockmen say. "No two are alike." The ideal of livestock breeding over the centuries has not been to produce clones. Recognition of "type" is certainly important. But paramount is the ability to recognize the outstanding individual.

The plainest and most emphatic denunciation of critical reductionism, and one that is generally ignored by critics, is the "Notice" posted at the beginning of *Huckleberry Finn:* "Persons attempting to find a motive in this narrative will be prosecuted; persons attempting to find a moral in it will be banished; persons attempting to find a plot in it will be shot." Mark Twain's point, I think, is not that his book had no motive or moral or plot, but rather that its motive, its moral, and its plot were peculiar to itself as a whole, and could be conveyed only by itself as a whole. The motive, the moral, and the plot were not to be extracted and studied piecemeal like the organs of a laboratory frog. And the reason for this is plain: The value of *Huckleberry Finn* is not in its motive or moral or plot, but in its language. The book is valuable because it is a story *told,* not a story explained.

Or the problem of reduction in art may be illustrated by the problem of translating a poem from one language to another. The problem is that the poetry is in the language, or is the language. We can certainly translate the "sense" of one language to another, but the question of how to translate a poem from one language to another is the same question as how to translate a language from one language to another, which cannot be done. And so translators of poetry must accept failure as the primary condition of their work. They must settle, at best, for second best: Their translations must succeed or fail as new poems in their own language which at the same time serve as approximations or shadows of the original poems. Nobody, I think, has ever believed that there was an equation between a translation and the original.

You cannot translate a poem into an explanation, any more than you can translate a poem into a painting or a painting into a piece of music or a piece of music into a walking stick. A work of art says what it says in the only way it can be said. Beauty, for example, cannot be interpreted. It is not an empirically verifiable fact; it is not a quantity. Artists and critics and teachers and students certainly ought to notice that some things are beautiful and some are not; they ought to ask, and learn if they can, the difference between beauty and ugliness; they should learn how beautiful things are made and how things are made beautiful; but they might as well not ask what are the equivalents of beauty in ideas or pulse rates or dollars or "ordinary language." To believe that the arts can be interpreted so as to make them consilient with biology or physics is about equivalent to the belief that literary classics can survive as comic books or movies.

The truth too, as it appears in art, cannot be extracted as an idea or paraphrase. If we didn't, to start with, feel that a work of art was true, we wouldn't bother with it, or not for long. I don't think we stand before Gerard David's *Annunciation,* in the Metropolitan Museum, as speculators of the truth. We don't say, Can this be true? or, Might it have happened this way? Either we see that in the painting it is happening, or we don't. If we don't, we pass on by. Of course, if we assent to the painting, and if we are responsible people, we finally must ask if it is true. We must measure it against our knowledge of other paintings and other visions of holy things. We must ask if we are being fooled, or are fooling ourselves. Nevertheless, the painting must be accepted or rejected as itself, not on the basis of interpretation or our opinion of Luke 1:28-35. The painting says what it says in the only way it can be said.

I don't mean at all to say that criticism is impossible, or that it cannot be useful. Obviously, we need to talk about works of art. We must test our ways of knowing about them. We must learn them and teach them and describe them and study the ways they are made. We must compare them with one another, and evaluate them by whatever standards we can make applicable. But a work of criticism is not equivalent to a work of art and cannot replace it. The English departments and the biology departments and all other would-be consilient departments can spend the next millennium interpreting *King Lear,* and at the end of all that work the interpretation will still be one kind of thing and *King Lear* will still be a thing of a different kind. And so Mr. Wilson's idea that the arts' "essential qualities of truth and beauty [can be] described through ordinary language" (p. 210) is not merely off the subject, as might first appear; it is a violation of sense. It is saying, in effect, that extraordinary language can be described in ordinary language. This is too flimsy a scaffold to hold up much in the way of art criticism.

The question remains, Is it science? If "science" means proven knowledge or a methodology for proving knowledge, then Mr. Wilson's chapter on "The Arts and Their Interpretation" is no closer to science than it is to art criticism. On page 218, he makes this startling confession: "Gene-culture coevolution is, I believe, the underlying process by which the brain evolved and the arts originated. It is the conceivable means most consistent with the joint findings of the brain sciences, psychology, and evolutionary biology. Still, *direct* evidence with reference to the arts is slender." On this "I believe," this "conceivable," and this "slender" evidence, Mr. Wilson's enormous speculation teeters, like the Balanced Rock. It is not a reassuring place for a picnic.

VI. A Conversation Out of School

THE DISCIPLINES are different from one another, each distinct in itself, and rightly so. Science and art are neither fundamental nor immutable. They are not life or the world. They are tools. The arts and the sciences are our kit of cultural tools. Science cannot replace art or religion for the same reason that you cannot loosen a nut with a saw or cut a board in two with a wrench. The first question about the disciplines is not how they originated but how and for what they are to be used.

But if the sciences and the arts are divided into "two cultures," or into many subcultures, they are nobody's kit of tools. They are not the subjects of one conversation. They cannot be used in collaboration. And if they cannot be gathered together in one culture by consilience—which, on the evidence of Mr. Wilson's book, is not probable—then what can gather them together?

The only reason, really, that we need this kit of tools is to build and maintain our dwelling here on earth. (Those who wish to live or do business in other worlds should be free to depart, but not to return.) Our dwelling here is the proper work of culture. If the tools can be used collaboratively, then maybe we can find what are the appropriate standards for our work and can then build a good and lasting dwelling—which actually would be a diversity of dwellings suited to the diversity of homelands. If the tools cannot be so used, then they will be used to destroy such dwellings as we have accomplished so far, and our homelands as well.

*

To begin to think of the possibility of collaboration among the disciplines, we must realize that the "two cultures" exist as such because both of them belong to the one culture of division and dislocation, opposition and competition, which is to say the culture of colonialism and industrialism. This culture has steadily increased the dependence of individuals, regions, and nations upon larger and larger collective economies at the same time that it has thrown individuals, regions, and nations into a competitiveness with one another that is limitlessly destructive and demeaning. This state of universal competition understands the world as an anti-pattern in which each thing is opposed to every other thing, and it destroys the self-sufficiency of all places—households, farms, communities, regions, nations—even as it destroys the self-sufficiency of the world.

The collective economy is run for the benefit of a decreasing number of increasingly wealthy corporations. These corporations understand their "global economy" as a producer of money, not of goods. The goods of the world such as topsoil or forests must decline so that the money may increase. To facilitate this process, the corporations patronize the disciplines, chiefly the sciences, but some of the money, as "philanthropy," trickles down upon the arts. The brokers of this patronage are the universities, which are the organizers of the disciplines in our time. Since the universities are always a-building and are always in need of money, they accept the economy's fundamental principle of the opposition of money to goods. Having thus accepted as real the world as an anti-pattern of competing opposites, it is merely inevitable that they should organize learning, not as a conversation of collaborating disciplines, but as an anti-system of opposed and competing divisions. They have departmented our one great responsibility to live ably and generously into a nest of irresponsibilities. The sciences are sectioned like a stockyard the better to serve the corporations. The so-called humanities, which might have supplied at least a corrective or chastening remembrance of the good that humans have sometimes accomplished, have been dismembered into utter fecklessness, turning out "communicators" who have nothing to say and "educators" who have nothing to teach.

Must we reconcile ourselves to this cultural disintegration, this cacophony of the disciplines? Is it possible, failing consilience, to bring the arts and the sciences into healthful coherence and community of purpose? Edward O. Wilson would like to consiliate art and science on the terms of science — wrongly, I believe. The correct response is not to substitute the terms of art, or to look about for some hardly imaginable compromise.

The correct response, I think, is to ask if science and art are inherently at odds with one another. It seems obvious that they are not. To see that they are not may require extracurricular thought, but once we have cracked the crust of academic convention we can see that "science" means knowing and that "art" means doing, and that one is meaningless without the other. Out of school, the two are commonly inter-involved and naturally cooperative in the same person—a farmer, say, or a woodworker—who knows and does, both at the same time. It may be more or less possible to know and do nothing, but it is not possible to do and know nothing. One does as one knows. It is not possible to imagine a farmer who does not use both science and art.

It is also obvious that there is no insuperable natural or inherent division between scientists and artists—at least there is none outside of the academic pigeonholes. It is possible for a scientist and an artist to take part in the same conversation. On this subject I can speak from experience. I have been for the greater part of my life an artist of sorts, a cottage industrialist of literature, and for the past nineteen years I have been involved in a conversation with Wes Jackson, who is a scientist, a plant geneticist, and co-founder of the Land Institute in Salina, Kansas. This conversation has been, from the beginning, an alliance and a friendship. To me, it has been an indispensable source of instruction and a continuous testing of my thoughts. I can't speak for Wes, of course, and I make no claims as to the quality of our talk; the point here is only that we have been able to talk to each other out of our supposedly estranged disciplines, making our disciplines in the process useful to one another. In many meetings, telephone calls, notes, and letters during nineteen years, we have almost always had questions, and sometimes have had answers, for each other.

One of the most interesting facts about our conversation, from the standpoint of this essay, is that we were not prepared for it by our schooling. Wes's Ph.D. in genetics and my M.A. in English were not designed to give us things to say to each other. Because of his knowledge of the Bible and various works of literature, Wes was better prepared to talk to me than I to talk to him. Before I met him, I had been for perhaps fifteen years under the influence of the writings of the English agricultural scientist, Sir Albert Howard, and this was all that enabled me to understand Wes's germinal idea that, to be enduring, agriculture must imitate the local processes of nature. Though Wes is a writer (we both are essayists), I am not a scientist. I am perfectly ignorant of some things that Wes knows perfectly. While I have been writing, in addition to essays about agriculture, a series of fragments of the history of an imagined rural community, Wes has been at work on a project to renew agriculture by the development of perennial grain crops, in imitation of the native prairie plant communities, thereby reducing the amount of plowing necessary for food production, thereby reducing our presently ruinous rates of soil erosion. Obviously, two men so divergently occupied, and so divided by education, cannot talk together by any notion of the unification or consilience of their disciplines. And so what has made our conversation possible? The list of reasons amounts in implication to a fairly complete criticism of the present organization of the disciplines and the assumptions of that organization:

1. Though Wes and I were specialized, and maybe too much so,

by our formal schooling, that schooling was superimposed upon an earlier, older education that we have in common. We both were raised in agrarian families. We were taught as children to know, respect, and love farming. From childhood until now, our thoughts about agriculture have been informed and conditioned by the actual work of farming, and this is work that we *like*.

2. Though we both have taught in universities, I more than Wes, neither of us has made a life in a university or in a "university community." We have lived in the countryside, among farming people, and have been involved in farming. In our minds, the problems we have talked about have always had the aspect of particular places and people, intimately known and cared about.

3. In ways sometimes different and sometimes the same, we have been at work on the same problem: how to change from a culture and a system of agriculture that destroy land and people to a culture and a system able to conserve both.

4. Because good land use involves both science and art (knowing and doing) and cannot be understood or practiced as either alone, we have had no illusions about the self-sufficiency or the adequacy of either of our disciplines. Our conversation has been between two parts of an always uncompleted whole. It has lasted so long partly, of course, because it has been enjoyable, but also because it has been necessary.

5. The questions that have concerned us have been the same, and all of them raise the most practical issues of propriety: How can land and people be well used? What is good use? What is good knowledge, good thought, good work? How can one become genuinely and honorably native to one's place? This last question (the

terms of which are set forth in Wes's book *Becoming Native to This Place*) is paramount. Asking it removes one permanently from the "two cultures" of careerist artists and scientists.

6. Neither of us believes that either art or science can be "neutral." Influence and consequence are inescapable. History continues. You cannot serve both God and Mammon, and you cannot work without serving one or the other.

7. Though each of us possesses the specialized vocabulary of his discipline, our conversation uses such talk only when necessary. We both can speak common English. Each of us, moreover, can speak a local English that is a source both of pleasure and exactitude. Our conversation is always striving to be local and particular. It is full of proper nouns, names of places and people. This subject of language is of the greatest importance, and I will have to return to it.

VII. Toward a Change of Standards

I HAVE JUST implied that a scientist and an artist may have to live and work outside the university if they are to have a sustained, mutually instructive, and effective conversation. Some will argue with this, and so be it. I will only point out that the modern university is organized to divide the disciplines; that universities pay little or no attention to the local and earthly effects of the work that is done in them; and that in the universities one discipline is rarely called upon to answer questions that might be asked of it by another discipline. If the universities sponsored an authentic conversation among the disciplines, then, for example, the colleges of agriculture would long ago have been brought under questioning by the college of arts and sciences or of medicine. A vital, functioning intellectual community *could* not sponsor patterns of land use that are increasingly toxic, violent, and destructive of rural communities.

I don't at all mean to suggest that I know how to reorganize the disciplines. I don't know how to do that, and I doubt that anybody does. But I feel no hesitation in saying that the standards and goals of the disciplines need to be changed. It used to be that we thought of the disciplines as ways of being useful to ourselves, for we needed to earn a living, but also and more importantly we thought of them as ways of being useful to one another. As long as the idea of vocation was still viable among us, I don't believe it was ever understood that a person was "called" to be rich or powerful or even successful. People were taught the disciplines at home or in school for two reasons: to enable them to live and work both as self-sustaining individuals and as useful members of their communities, and to see that the disciplines themselves survived the passing of the generations.

Now we seem to have replaced the ideas of responsible community membership, of cultural survival, and even of usefulness, with the idea of professionalism. Professional education proceeds according to ideas of professional competence and according to professional standards, and this explains the decline in education from ideals of service and good work, citizenship and membership, to mere "job training" or "career preparation." The context of professionalism is not a place or a community but a career, and this explains the phenomenon of "social mobility" and all the evils that proceed from it. The religion of professionalism is progress, and this means that, in spite of its vocal bias in favor of practicality and realism, professionalism forsakes both past and present in favor of the future, which is never present or practical or real. Professionalism is always offering up the past and the present as sacrifices to the future, in which all our problems will be solved and our tears wiped away—and which, being the future, never arrives. The future is always free of past limitations and present demands, always stocked with newer merchandise than any presently available, always promising that what we are going to have is better than what we have. The future is the utopia of academic thought, for virtually anything is hypothetically possible there; and it is the always-expanding frontier of the industrial economy, the fictive real estate against which losses are debited and to which failures are exiled. The future is not anticipated or provided for, but is only bought or sold. The present is ever diminished by this buying and selling of shares in the future that rightfully are owned by the unborn.

*

Wallace Stegner knew, both from his personal experience and from his long study of his region, that the two cultures of the American West are not those of the sciences and the arts, but rather those of the two human kinds that he called "boomers" and "stickers," the boomers being "those who pillage and run," and the stickers "those who settle, and love the life they have made and the place they have made it in" (*Where the Bluebird Sings to the Lemonade Springs,* p. xxii). This applies to our country as a whole, and maybe to all of Western civilization in modern times. The first boomers were the oceanic navigators of the European Renaissance. They were gold seekers. All boomers have been gold seekers. They are would-be Midases who want to turn all things into gold: plants and animals, trees, food and drink, soil and water and air, life itself, even the future.

The sticker theme has so far managed to survive, and to preserve in memory and even in practice the ancient human gifts of reverence, fidelity, neighborliness, and stewardship. But unquestionably the dominant theme of modern history has been that of the boomer. It is no surprise that the predominant arts and sciences of the modern era have been boomer arts and boomer sciences.

The collaboration of boomer science with the boomer mentality of the industrial corporations has imposed upon us a state of virtually total economy in which it is the destiny of every creature (humans not excepted) to have a price and to be sold. In a total economy, all materials, creatures, and ideas become commodities, interchangeable and disposable. People become commodities along with everything else. Only such an economy could seek to impose upon the world's abounding geographic and creaturely diversity the tyranny of technological and genetic monoculture. Only in such an economy could "life forms" be patented, or the renewability of nature and culture be destroyed. Monsanto's aptly named "terminator gene"—which, implanted in seed sold by Monsanto, would cause the next generation of seed to be sterile—is as grave an indicator of totalitarian purpose as a concentration camp.

The complicity of the arts and humanities in this conquest is readily apparent in the enthusiasm with which the disciplines, schools, and libraries have accepted their ever-growing dependence (at public expense) on electronic technologies that are, in fact, as all of history shows, not necessary to learning or teaching, and which have produced no perceptible improvement in either. This was accomplished virtually without a dissenting voice, without criticism, without regard even for the economic cost. It is the clearest demonstration so far that the cult of originality and innovation is in fact a crowd of conformists, tramping on one another's heels for fear of being the last to buy whatever is for sale.

With the same ardor, and in more or less the same stampede, this crowd has mastered a slang of personal "liberation" that has done little for real freedom (which requires perception of authentic differences and distinctions), but has set many free from their rightful obligations and responsibilities—to, for example, their spouses and their children. The arts, especially in their well-paying popular versions, have become adept as permission givers for this sort of freedom. But there is too close a kinship between the personal freedom from reverence, fidelity, neighborliness, and stewardship and the corporate freedom to pollute and exterminate. When, if ever, the accounting is properly done, many of our present "liberties" and "necessities" will be seen to owe too much to the exploitation of "cheap" labor, raw materials, energy, and food.

The dominant story of our age, undoubtedly, is that of adultery and divorce. This is true both literally and figuratively: The dominant *tendency* of our age is the breaking of faith and the making of divisions among things that once were joined. This story obviously must be told by somebody. Perhaps, in one form or another, it must be told (because it must be experienced) by everybody. But how has it been told, and how ought it be told? This is a critical question, but not a question merely for art criticism. The story can be told in a way that clarifies, that makes imaginable and compassionable, the suffering and the costs; or it can be told in a way that seems to grant an easy permission and absolution to adultery and divorce. Can literature, for example, be written according to standards that are not merely literary? Obviously it can. And it had better be.

*

Suppose, then, that we should change the standards, as in fact some scientists and some artists already are attempting to do. Suppose that the ultimate standard of our work were to be, not professionalism and profitability, but the health and durability of human and natural communities. Suppose we learned to ask of any proposed innovation the question that so far only the Amish have been wise enough to ask: What will this do to our community? Suppose we attempted the authentic multiculturalism of adapting our ways of life to the nature of the places where we live. Suppose, in short, that we should take seriously the proposition that our arts and sciences have the power to help us adapt and survive. What then?

Well, we certainly would have a healthier, prettier, more diverse and interesting world, a world less toxic and explosive, than we have now.

And how might this come about? Again, I have to say that I don't know. I don't like or trust large, official programs of improvement, and I don't want to appear to be inviting any such thing. But perhaps there is no harm in making suggestions, if I acknowledge that the suggestions are only mine, and if I make sure that my suggestions apply primarily to the thinking, work, and conduct of individuals. Here is my list:

1. Rather than the present economic hierarchy of the professions, which results in the denigration and undercompensation of essential jobs of work, particularly in the economies of land use, we should think and work toward an appropriate subordination of all the disciplines to the health of creatures, places, and communities. A science or an art, for example, that served settlement rather than the exploitation of "frontiers" would be subordinate to reverence, fidelity, neighborliness, and stewardship, to affection and delight. It would aim to keep our creatureliness intact.

2. We should banish from our speech and writing any use of the word "machine" as an explanation or definition of anything that is not a machine. Our understanding of creatures and our use of them are *not* improved by calling them machines.

3. We should abandon the idea that this world and our human life in it can be brought by science to some sort of mechanical perfection or predictability. We are creatures whose intelligence and knowledge are not invariably equal to our circumstances. The radii of knowledge have only pushed back—and enlarged—the circumference of mystery. We live in a world famous for its ability both to surprise us and to deceive us. We are prone to err, ignorantly or foolishly or intentionally or maliciously. One of the oddest things about us is the interdependency of our virtues and our faults. Our moral code depends on our shortcomings as much as our knowledge. It is only when we confess our ignorance that we can see our need for "the law and the prophets." It is only because we err and are ignorant that we make promises, which we keep, not because we are smart, but because we are faithful.

4. We should give up the frontier and its boomer "ethics" of greed, cunning, and violence, and, so near too late, accept settlement as our goal. Wes Jackson says that our schools now have only one major, upward mobility, and that we need to offer a major in homecoming. I agree, and would only add that a part of the sense of "homecoming" must be home*making,* for we now must begin sometimes with remnants, sometimes with ruins.

5. We need to require from our teachers, researchers, and leaders —and attempt for ourselves—a responsible accounting of technological progress. What have we gained by computers, for example, *after* we have subtracted the ecological costs of making them, using them, and throwing them away, the value of lost time and work when "the computers are down," and the enormous economic cost of the "Y2K" correction?

6. We ought conscientiously to reduce our tolerance for ugliness. Why, if we are in fact "progressing," should so much expense and effort have resulted in so much ugliness? We ought to begin to ask ourselves what are the limits—of scale, speed, and probably expense as well—beyond which human work is bound to be ugly.

7. We should recognize the insufficiency, to our life here among living creatures, of the abstract categories of reductionist thought. Resist classification! Without some use of abstraction, thought is incoherent or unintelligible, perhaps unthinkable. But abstraction alone is merely dead. And here we return again to the crucial issue of language.

In our public dialogue (such as it is) we are now using many valuable words that are losing their power of reference, and have as a consequence become abstract, merely gestures. I have in mind words such as "patriotism," "freedom," "equality," and "rights," or "nature," "human," "wild," and "sustainable." We could make a longish list of words such as these, which we often use without thought or feeling, just to show which side we suppose we want to be on. This situation calls for language that is not sloganish and rhetorical, but rather is capable of reference, specification, precision, and refinement—a language never far from experience and example. In the work of the great poets, the heavenly and the earthly are not abstract, but are *present;* the language of those poets is whole and precise. We are mistaken to think that we can increase our earthly knowledge by ignoring Heaven, or become more intelligent by giving up Dante or condescending to Milton. The middling, politically correct language of the professions is incapable either of reverence or familiarity; it is headless and footless, loveless, a language of nowhere.

I believe that this need for a whole, vital, particularizing language applies just as strongly to the sciences as to the arts and humanities. For the human necessity is not just to know, but also to cherish and protect the things that are known, and to know the things that can be known only by cherishing. If we are to protect the world's multitude of places and creatures, then we must know them, not just conceptually but imaginatively as well. They must be pictured in the mind and in memory; they must be known with affection, "by heart," so that in seeing or remembering them the heart may be said to "sing," to make a music peculiar to its recognition of each particular place or creature that it knows well. I am remembering here the importance to Confucius of "the tones given off by the heart" (Ezra Pound, *Confucius,* pp. 31, 47). To know imaginatively is to know intimately, particularly, precisely, gratefully, reverently, and with affection.

In *Consilience,* Edward O. Wilson says, "Today the entire planet has become home ground" (p. 233), but that is a conceptual statement only, and doubtful as such. No human has ever known, let alone imagined, the entire planet. And even in an age of "world travel," none of us lives on the entire planet; in fact, owing to so much mobility, a lot of people (as some of them will tell you) don't live anywhere. But if we are to know any part of the planet intimately, particularly, precisely, and with affection, then we must live somewhere in particular for a long time. We must be able to call up to the mind's eye by name a lot of local places, people, creatures, and things.

One of the most significant costs of the economic destruction of farm populations is the loss of local memory, local history, and local names. Field names, for instance, even such colorless names as "the front field" and "the back field," are vital signs of a culture. If the arts and the sciences ever waken from their rapture of academic specialization, they will make themselves at home in places they have helped to spoil, and set about reconstructing histories and remembering names.

8. We should value familiarity above innovation. Boomer scientists and artists want to discover (so to speak) a place where they have not been. Sticker scientists and artists want to know where

they are. There is no reason that familiarity cannot be a goal just as worthy, demanding, and exciting as innovation—or, as I would argue, much more so. It would certainly give worthwhile employment to more people. And in fact its boundaries are much larger. Innovation is limited always by human ingenuity and human means; familiarity is limited only by the limits of life. The real infinitude of experience is in familiarity.

My own experience has shown me that it is possible to live in and attentively study the same small place decade after decade, and find that it ceaselessly evades and exceeds comprehension. There is nothing that it can be reduced to, because "it" is always, and not predictably, changing. It is never the same two days running, and the better one pays attention the more aware one becomes of these differences. Living and working in the place day by day, one is continuously revising one's knowledge of it, continuously being surprised by it and in error about it. And even if the place stayed the same, one would be getting older and growing in memory and experience, and would need for that reason alone to work from revision to revision. One knows one's place, that is to say, only within limits, and the limits are in one's mind, not in the place. This is a description of life in time in the world. A place, apart from our now always possible destruction of it, is inexhaustible. It *cannot* be altogether known, seen, understood, or appreciated.

That Cézanne returned many times to paint Mont Sainte-Victoire, or that William Carlos Williams spent a long life writing about Rutherford, New Jersey, does not mean that those places are now exhausted as subjects. It means that they are inexhaustible. There are many examples of this. One that I have kept in mind for nearly forty years, to define a hope and a consolation, is that of the French entomologist, Jean Henri Fabre. Too poor to travel, Fabre spent the last thirty-odd years of his life studying the insects and other creatures of his small *harmas* near Sérignan, "a patch of pebbles enclosed within four walls" (Edwin Way Teale, *The Insect World of J. Henri Fabre*, p. 2). And surely his enthusiasm lasted so long because he studied the living creatures in their—and his—dwelling place.

There is nothing intrinsically wrong with an interest in discovery and innovation. It only becomes wrong when it is thought to be the norm of culture and of intellectual life. As such it is in the first place misleading. As I have already suggested, the effort of familiarity is always leading to discovery and the new, just as do the quests of explorers and "original researchers." The difference is that innovation for its own sake, and especially now when it so directly serves the market, is disruptive of human settlement, whereas the revelations of familiarity elaborate the local cultural pattern and tend toward settlement, which they also prevent from becoming static.

If local adaptation is important, as I believe it unquestionably is, then we must undertake, in both science and art, the effort of familiarity. In doing so, we will confront the endlessness of human knowledge, work, and experience. But we should not mislead ourselves: We will confront mystery too. There is more to the world, and to our own work in it, than we are going to know.

One of the best studies of local adaptation that I know is a book by George Sturt, *The Wheelwright's Shop* (Cambridge, 1980), which looks at traditional farm carts and wagons as products of "the age-long effort of Englishmen to fit themselves close and ever closer into England" (p. 66). Sturt understands these vehicles as distinctly local products, whose form and fabric evolved in a long, only partly conscious give and take between the people and the landscape. The accommodation inherent in the design was elegant, though not in any sure sense explainable:

"But where begin to describe so efficient an organism, in which all the parts interacted until it is hard to say which was modified first, to meet which other? Was it to suit the horses or the ruts, the loading or the turning, that the front wheels had to have a diameter of about four feet? Or was there something in the average height of a carter, or in the skill of wheel-makers, that fixed these dimensions? One only knew that, by a wonderful compromise, all these points had been provided for in the country tradition of forewheels for a waggon. And so all through. Was it to suit these same wheels that the front of a waggon was slightly curved up, or was that done in consideration of the loads, and the circumstance merely taken advantage of for the wheels? I could not tell. I cannot tell. I only know that in these and a hundred details every well-built farm-waggon (of whatever variety) was like an organism, reflecting in every curve and dimension some special need of its own country-side, or, perhaps, some special difficulty attending wheelwrights with the local timber" (pp. 66-67).

This is the way a locally adapted culture works. Over a long time it learns to conform its artifacts to the local landscape, local circumstances, and local needs. This is exactly opposite to the way of industrialism, which forces the locality to conform to its artifacts, always with the most dreadful consequences to the locality. Having in the industrial age exchanged, as Sturt says, "local needs . . . for cosmopolitan wishes" (p. 75), we are a long way now from the saving elegance that his book recalls. And the most resolute and expensive projects of discovery and innovation on the part of science-technology-and-industry cannot take us there. Only a long, patient, loving effort of familiarity can do that.

Hanging his project from an "if," as usual, Edward O. Wilson looks forward to "a Magellanic voyage that eventually encircles the whole of reality" (*Consilience,* p. 268). This presumably will be the long end run that will carry us and "the environment" over the goal line of survival.

But in an earlier book, *Biophilia,* Mr. Wilson set forth a far different conclusion, one which he has now evidently repudiated, but which I wish to affirm: "That the naturalist's journey has only begun and for all intents and purposes will go on forever. That it is possible to spend a lifetime in a magellanic voyage around the trunk of a single tree" (p. 22).

A single tree? Well, life is a miracle and therefore infinitely of interest everywhere. We have perhaps sufficient testimony, from artists and scientists both, that if we watch, refine our intelligence and our attention, curb our greed and our pride, work with care, have faith, a single tree might be enough.

IN THE PROCESS that carries knowledge from the laboratory to the market there is not enough fear. And in the history of that process there has not been adequate accounting.

Richard Strohman has made clear what is objectionable about the infusion of money from biotechnology corporations into the universities: These grants will press university scientists in the direction of product development; an interest in product development increases the emphasis upon predictability (you cannot market, or not for long, an unpredictable product); but an undue emphasis upon predictability will tend to narrow the context of experimentation, making the product, in the context of the world, unpredictable in effect and influence (*The Daily Californian,* April 1, 1999, p. 5; and *The Wild Duck Review,* Summer 1999, pp. 27-29).

This process has a historical analogue in the introduction of the internal combustion engine into agriculture. In the commercial workshops tractors had only to pass the test of mechanical correctness: They had to start and run more or less predictably. In the context of the world, however, these machines had effects and exerted influences that far surpassed their merely mechanical limits. They replaced agriculture's old dependence on the free energy of the sun with a dependence on purchased energy; in general, they increased farming's dependence on a supply economy that farmers cannot control or influence; over the years, these dependences have radically oversimplified the patterns of farming, replacing diversity with monoculture, crop rotation with continuous tillage, and human labor with machines and chemicals; they have replaced (in Wes Jackson's words) nature's wisdom with human cleverness; they have caused widespread, profound social and cultural disruption. All these changes are still in progress. Whatever the technological or quantitative gains, this industrialization of farming has been costly, and it will continue to be. Most of the costs have been "externalized"—that is, charged to nature or the public or the future.

The response to this in the land grant universities has been applause.

*

The faculties and administrations of universities are inexcusably bewildered between the superstition that knowledge is invariably good and the fact that it can be monetarily valuable and also dangerous.

There is in fact no reason to think that the professions are self-correcting, or that new knowledge necessarily compensates for old error.

*

The time is past, if ever there was such a time, when you can just discover knowledge and turn it loose in the world and assume that you have done good.

This, to me, is a sign of the incompleteness of science in itself—which is a sign of the need for a strenuous conversation among all the branches of learning. This is a conversation that the universities have failed to produce, and in fact have obstructed.

*

If we were as fearful of our knowledge and our power as in our ignorance we ought to be—and as our cultural and religious traditions instruct us to be—then we would be trying to reconnect the disciplines both within the universities and in the conduct of the professions.

*

In our present economic predicament, ethics, ecology, environmental law, etc. won't *as specialties* have much corrective force. They will be used to rationalize what is wrong.

*

The anti-smoking campaign, by its insistent reference to the expensiveness to government and society of death by smoking, has raised a question that it has not answered: What is the best and cheapest disease to die from, and how can the best and cheapest disease best be promoted?

*

An idea of health that does not generously and gracefully accommodate the fact of death is obviously incomplete. The crudest manifestation of modern medicine is its routine, stubborn, and finally cruel resistance to death. This comes of the refusal to accept death not only as part of health, which it demonstrably is, but also as a great mystery both in itself and as a part of the mystery that surrounds us all our lives. The medical industry's resistance is only sometimes an instance of scientific heroism; sometimes it is the fear of what we don't know anything about.

*

Science can teach us and help us to resist death, but it can't teach us to prepare for death or to die well.

The question of how you want to die is somewhat fantastical but nonetheless it is one that all the living need to consider, one that belongs to the issue of health, and one that health science can't answer.

Do you want to die at home with your people "in blessed peace around you," which is the death Tiresias foresaw for Odysseus and the one Homer seems to recommend?

Or do you want to die in the hands of the best medical professionals wherever they are?

Such questions may seem irrelevant until you realize that they define two very different lives.

*

The refusal of modern medicine to confront the deaths of its patients is only a function of its refusal to confront the unique and unempirically precious lives of its patients.

Analogous to that is modern agriculture's refusal to confront the life of a good or healthy farm as a cultural artifact, unique in place and character, complex in form, mysterious in its sources, and many times more fascinating and precious than the "unit of production" to which it has been reduced by the economics of "agribusiness" and the colleges of agriculture.

*

My worry is only partly about science-as-Pandora, an activity of questioning or curiosity which cannot undo the harm that it may do and sometimes does. (Science has armed us but it cannot disarm us.)

I am worried also about the *application* of science, which I think is generally crude. This cannot be solved merely by keeping the context of research as large as it actually is in application — which, of course, would be a sensible precaution. However large the context, however generous the acknowledgment of context, the results of the research still cannot be applied *both* generally and sensitively. Finally it is "brought home" to a specific community of persons and creatures in a specific place. If it is then applied in its abstract or generalized or marketable form, it will obscure the uniquenesses of the subject persons or creatures or places, or of their community, and this sort of application is almost invariably destructive.

The only remedy I can see is for scientists (and artists also) to understand and imagine themselves as members of, and sharers in, the fate of affected communities. Our schools now encourage people to regard as mere privileges the power and influence that they call leadership. But leadership without membership is a terrible thing.

*

The issue of the application of science is a political issue. If the science is applied only by, or can only be applied by, a government or a large corporation, then it is tyrannical. If it is to be applied, it should be applied locally by local people on a local scale, using the health of the locality as the standard of application and judgment.

The use of science by or upon people who do not understand it is always potentially tyrannical, and it is always dangerous.

*

Applying knowledge—scientific or otherwise—is an art. An artist is somebody who knows what to put where, and when to put it. A good artist is one who applies knowledge skillfully and sensitively to the particular creatures and places of the world. Good farmers and good architects and good doctors are the most obvious examples, but the same potential is in all the arts. This is why it is such a shame to see the so-called fine arts elaborating themselves as academic or professional specialties without reference to much of anything, perhaps in imitation of the supposedly pure sciences.

*

The modern scientific enterprise apparently is directed toward the goal of complete knowledge. But if you had complete knowledge, if you knew everything, could you then act? Could you apply what you knew, or would you be paralyzed by a surplus of considerations? If you were to map within a circle all possible relationships among all the points along its circumference, you would end up with a black circle—an engorgement of "information" that would not be knowledge, but rather the practical equivalent of the blank circle you began with.

Thus the proposition that it would be good to know everything is probably false. The real question that is always to be addressed is the one that arises from our state of ignorance: How does one act well—sensitively, compassionately, without irreparable damage—on the basis of *partial* knowledge?

Perhaps the most proper, and the most natural, response to our state of ignorance is not haste to increase the amount of available information, or even to increase knowledge, but rather a lively and convivial engagement with the issues of form, elegance, and kindness. These issues of "sustainability" are both scientific and artistic.

*

The problem that we confront in our sciences and arts, as I understand it, is not a problem of information but a problem of ignorance. Or, to put it another way, the problem is not primarily one of mass; it is a problem of form.

It is out of our confrontation with our ignorance that we come to the problem of form. The ignorant must hope, and with study they may come to know, that it is possible to achieve forms that partake of wholeness and even holiness and make sense, even though one does not know everything.

*

Good artists are people who can stick things together so that they stay stuck. They know how to gather things into formal arrangements that are intelligible, memorable, and lasting. Good forms confer health upon the things that they gather together. Farms, families, and communities are forms of art just as are poems, paintings, and symphonies. None of these things would exist if we did not make them. We can make them either well or poorly; this choice is another thing that we make.

*

Always informing our practice of artistic form is our sense of the formality of creation. This "sense" is not knowledge of the empirical or scientific sort. It does not tend toward any sort of description. It is the perfectly assimilated, perfectly forgotten knowledge by which all creatures live in their places.

*

Overhanging all our thought and work is the question of how certain of itself human knowledge can be.

I learned from the theologian Philip Sherrard to ask this question: If things are evolving, and if human consciousness is evolving along with everything else, where do we find a standpoint from which to understand the whole process? (*Human Image: World Image*, Golgonooza Press, Ipswich, 1992, p. 72.)

To make the same point in a more practical way, let us take that ubiquitous and misleading word "environment"—which, as used, proposes that reality is composed of a creature and its surroundings. But if, as in fact we know, the creature is not only *in* its environment but *of* it, and if the relationship between creature and environment is mutually formative, and if this relationship is a process that cannot be stopped short of the creature's death, then how can we get outside the relationship in order to predict with certainty the effects of our participation?

Religion begins with such questions. But even reason can see that they define the issues of propriety and scale. If we can't know with final certainty what we are doing, then reason cautions us to be humble and patient, to keep the scale small, to be careful, to go slow.

*

In speaking of the reductionism of modern science, we should not forget that the primary reductionism is in the assumption that human experience or human meaning can be adequately represented in any human language. This assumption is false.

To show what I mean, I will give the example that is most immediate to my mind:

My grandson, who is four years old, is now following his father and me over some of the same countryside that I followed my father and grandfather over. When his time comes, my grandson will choose as he must, but so far all of us have been farmers. I know from my grandfather that when he was a child he too followed his father in this way, hearing and seeing, not knowing yet that the most essential part of his education had begun.

And so in this familiar spectacle of a small boy tagging along behind his father across the fields, we are part of a long procession, five generations of which I have seen, issuing out of generations lost to memory, going back, for all I know, across previous landscapes and the whole history of farming.

Modern humans tend to believe that whatever is known can be recorded in books or on tapes or on computer discs and then again learned by those artificial means.

But it is increasingly plain to me that the meaning, the cultural significance, even the practical value, of this sort of family procession across a landscape can be known but not told. These things, though they have a public value, do not have a public meaning; they are too specific to a particular small place and its history. This is exactly the tragedy in the modern displacement of people and cultures.

That such things can be known but not told can be shown by answering a simple question: *Who* knows the meaning, the cultural significance, and the practical value of this rural family's generational procession across its native landscape? The answer is not so simple as the question: No one person ever will know all the answer. My grandson certainly does not know it. And my son does not, though he has positioned himself to learn some of it, should he be so blessed.

I am the one who (to some extent) knows, though I know also that I cannot tell it to anyone living. I am in the middle now between my grandfather and my father, who are alive in my memory, and my son and my grandson, who are alive in my sight.

If my son, after thirty more years have passed, has the good pleasure of seeing his own child and grandchild in that procession, then he will know something like what I now know.

This living procession through time in a place *is* the record by which such knowledge survives and is conveyed. When the procession ends, so does the knowledge.